Warrior Principles

HARNESSING THE POWER OF RESILIENCE

JULIE LAWSON

Warrior Principles
Harnessing the Power of Resilience
Julie Lawson
Auburn Media

Published by Auburn Media, St. Louis, MO
Copyright ©2022 Julie Lawson
All rights reserved.

Editor: Cheryl Oliver

Cover and Interior design: Davis Creative Publishing Partners, CreativePublishingPartners.com

Names: Lawson, Julie, 1975- author.
Title: Warrior principles : harnessing the power of resilience / Julie Lawson.
Description: St. Louis, MO : Auburn Media, [2022] | Includes bibliographical references.
Identifiers: ISBN: 979-8-9869364-0-6 (paperback) | 979-8-9869364-1-3 (ebook) | LCCN: 2022916980
Subjects: LCSH: Resilience (Personality trait) | Stress management. | Job stress. | Success. | Success in business. | Psychology, Industrial. | LCGFT: Self-help publications. | BISAC: BUSINESS & ECONOMICS / Leadership. | SELF-HELP / Personal Growth / General. | BUSINESS & ECONOMICS / Personal Success.
Classification: LCC: BF698.35.R47 L39 2022 | DDC: 155.24--dc23
    2022

To all victims of crime, violence, war, and circumstance whose brilliant resilience inspires others to overcome, thrive, and find new joy. The hope of the world is yours.

ACKNOWLEDGEMENTS

This book would not be possible without the help and contributions of so many people. First, to all those whom I have had the pleasure of working with over the course of my career who have overcome remarkable odds: thank you for your spirit and resilience. You have seeded me and many others with a lifetime of inspiration.

Thank you to my mother, Janet, and my father, Jay, for their unconditional love and support, and for instilling resilience in me at a young age. You made it possible for me to have faith in the impossible.

To my siblings John, Joanne, and Jeff, my nieces and nephews (I love you each to pieces!) and all my family members: you give me purpose.

Thank you to amazing friends who boost me just when I need it: you teach me every day the power others have in my personal resilience. To mentors who inspire me to be a better person, and colleagues who challenge me to be my best, I am grateful. And finally, to Elmer, for your relentless encouragement and support for this book. It would not have been possible without you. Thank you for being my greatest champion.

I love you all and am infinitely grateful to have you in my life.

CONTENTS

EXERCISE INDEX

PREFACE

WHAT'S WITH THE PENGUIN?

The words "resilience" and "warrior" conjure a variety of images: a sword or shield, a soldier of ancient times clad in helmet and armor, or a fearless animal such as the lion. It elicits words such as "fierce," "mighty," "persevering." It does not make us think of a cute, happy penguin waddling innocently through life.

But it should. The penguin is one of the most resilient creatures on earth. Its ability to withstand tremendous adversity is remarkable: unthinkably cold temperatures, fierce winds, limited food supply, and predators challenge the penguin daily.

They are not fierce in appearance. They do not roar or fight. Instead, they use the power of community to ward off predators, withstand cruel winds, and raise future generations. The penguin has mastered the art of flexibly adapting to its harsh environment, embracing changes in temperature and food supply with ease. It gets through the challenges of daily life one small, persevering step at a time.

We are not resilient because we are physically strong, stoic, or aggressive. Like the penguin, we are resilient when we adapt to our world with ease and grace. When we can embrace our truest selves, happily navigating life as an integral part of our community.

Be a true warrior of resilience. **Be like the penguin.**

INTRODUCTION

My Story

Like many of us, my story begins not at my birth, but with powerful memories of moments that define or change us. These are our sparks of inspiration, our belly-laughs, the raw pain of humanness, the breathless gifts of love, and the grit of courage.

I have had many of these moments throughout my life, but one in particular began my life-long obsession with understanding what makes us resilient. I have dedicated decades to understanding what resilience looks like, how we get there, and how I can help unleash the warrior that lives in of each of us.

In 1998 I was assaulted by two men in rural Missouri. While I won't go into details, this experience was obviously a significant pivot point in my life. That day ripped through the cloth of my life in a blink, sentencing me to a life forever changed. I was unsure how I would navigate going forward and curious how I could trust the human condition again.

Unable to make sense of anything in my new world, I wandered for weeks through the halls of my mind seeking respite, understanding, and forgiveness. I quit my job, moved across state, and broke off my engagement. I tried to distract myself by being around others. Then I spent overwhelming hours alone. I worked out excessively. Then I laid still for days. I slept with the lights on. I slept on the couch. Then I slept during the day at work because I wasn't sleeping at night. I read the Bible and dozens of other religious texts while damning a God who had, in my shortsighted opinion, abandoned me (He had not). But mostly, I did everything I could to avoid healing. To plow through to tomorrow, hoping the experience would eventually just sort of drift away. Unsurprisingly, none of these steps changed how I felt or accelerated my healing. I learned over time that there is no way to get around this kind of experience. Through is the only option. Through is hard. It is relentless, exhausting, and overwhelming. And it is where we discover our resilience.

Like me, most of you have experienced a single moment that changed everything: the death of a loved one, a life-threatening illness, an accident that made you feel all-too-mortal. Whatever your story, you felt the walls of uncertainty and grief closing in around you. You, too, didn't know if or how tomorrow would come. You wondered if you'd have the grit to make it through or if you'd be afforded the grace you deserved afterwards. You felt overwhelmed by the magnitude of your circumstances. You felt like you might be the only person, ever or anywhere, to feel the way you do. You wondered if you have what it takes to survive.

And maybe, like me, that event became something that made you want to change the world, use your voice, or build something new. My assault led me to seek new ways to understand humanity and heal those in pain. It led me to a career assisting victims of violence and crisis, an honor I now can't imagine my life without. Through my work with victims, communities, and leaders, I have had the privilege of meeting hundreds of survivors of horrific crimes, disaster, debilitating illnesses, business and financial catastrophes, family tragedies and more—and all of them survived by igniting their resilience.

I am glad to say that, over time and with the help of amazing people, including my family, friends, and professionals, I healed from my experience and have woven it into the tapestry of my complex, wonderful, and blessed life. In 2005, I joined the oldest victim service agency in the nation, the Crime Victim Advocacy Center, as their President & CEO (at the time of publishing this book, I serve as the President of the Board of Directors). My time in this role, as well as in subsequent roles training and developing leaders, led me to discover how we can tap into our resilient nature to build a stronger world.

In the decades that followed my assault I worked with hundreds of victims who helped me identify, research, and confirm the characteristics that create resilience. When I moved into leadership development, I tested these same characteristics and discovered they also built strong, resilient, and fulfilled leaders. From these characteristics I developed the principles in this book, and I help organizations identify how to adapt these principles into their business strategies. This book is based on the research I, and my team, have conducted: interviews, discussions, surveys, trainings, evaluations, and studies into how thousands of individuals and groups build resilience. It is the culmination of 20 years of research into identifying and understanding the specific and unchangeable characteristics that make us resilient. The principles outlined in this book are the timeless, proven methods to becoming our strongest selves.

I have trained more than 5,000 leaders, created and built three companies, worked with the criminal justice system to tackle issues of racial and ethnic inequities, assisted countless social service agencies in building capacity to serve communities, and consulted with dozens of companies and government offices on how to build a resilient workforce. In 2017 I founded Reins Institute, a company dedicated to customized leadership development programming, training, and coaching, and continue to serve as its CEO today. Through these amazing experiences I confirmed what true resilience looks like and am now dedicated to sharing these concepts and methods with you. My goal, and my life's work, is to help you discover and ignite your strongest self.

Thank you for taking this journey with me.

PRINCIPLE ONE:

YOUR COMFORT ZONE IS NOT A DESTINATION

Our deepest fear is not that we are inadequate.
Our deepest fear is that we are powerful beyond measure.

—Marianne Williamson

Fear is a Liar

Renee[1] was 47 years old when she hired me as her coach. A marketing executive with exceptional credentials, she should have been in the prime of her career. To colleagues she appeared happy and confident. Internally, however, she felt like a failure. She knew she wasn't living up to her full potential and struggled to achieve even the most basic professional goals she set for herself.

Despite holding visible roles with substantial responsibility, Renee continually underperformed at each. She lamented a lifetime of unachieved goals, missed deadlines, disappointing feedback, and substandard work. She had the talent, experience, and knowledge to perform each job to its fullest, yet found herself repeatedly failing at her job. Finally, after 26 years of moves and promotions, she was fired from her dream job. Defeated, she came to me to discover why she continued to fail at the positions she loved and desperately wanted to succeed in.

"I am clearly afraid of failure," she explained.

"But you've failed many times and lived through it," I countered. "If you were afraid of failing, wouldn't you do everything to avoid it? I'm not sure that's the problem. What if, instead, you're afraid of success?"

I waited. She hadn't considered this idea until now. I asked her to identify what "success" meant to her: how would she feel if she considered herself successful? What would it make possible for her? How would it change the way she behaved, thought, or viewed the world?

---

1 Names have been changed to protect the identity of clients

I then asked her to remember a time in her life when she was truly, by anyone's definition, successful. She recalled a time in her mid-twenties when she was given a promotion based on her ability to masterfully manage key clients. She thrived on her new responsibility, working extra hours, attending a post-graduate class to sharpen her skills, and offering to help colleagues so she could learn more about a variety of job functions. Most importantly, she was happy and fulfilled.

"What happened then?" I asked. "My success destroyed everything," she said, with a tone of surprise.

In a long-term relationship with her college boyfriend, her new salary was enough for the couple to consider marriage. An engagement soon followed her promotion. Her fiancé, a fellow marketing professional, understood the growth potential of her new position and was initially happy and supportive. Slowly, however, he began to show contempt for her work responsibilities. He complained about his lesser salary, no longer showed up to important events she asked him to attend, and even accused her of having been promoted only because she was a woman. The relationship finally collapsed when she discovered he had been secretly dating someone else.

Though many years had passed, Renee began to recognize it as a key turning point in her mindset. Success was not a reward; it was a punishment. It led to the loss of someone she loved. Success began to represent jealousy, condemnation, betrayal, and pain: something to be avoided, not embraced. Fear convinced her that failure was a safer option. I asked her to then describe for me what failure brought her. Was it easier than success? Which did she prefer? Which resulted in the better outcome?

Renee was learning a crucial life lesson: **fear is a liar.** It makes us believe in only one solution, one lonely option, one disappointing outcome. It suggests we can make only right or wrong choices (and that any pain or struggle experienced by a choice indicates we made the wrong one). It whispers just enough self-doubt into our conscience that we abandon alternative choices or behaviors that may lead us out of our pain.

The truth is that every decision—every choice—has consequences. Even inaction is an action. The more important the decision, the more consequences we may experience. No matter the direction we choose, our decisions bring both joy and pain. Our only responsibility to ourselves is to choose what we believe will provide us the best outcome. Renee finally chose the path that she believed would bring her the most joy: working hard until she met her own expectations of success.

Renee, like many of us, behaved in ways that would set her up for what she said she didn't want, yet refused to behave differently when given a new opportunity. She was not proactive in changing what made her miserable. Because failure and underperformance were familiar to her. **It was her comfort zone.** Whatever the negative experience, the result will be the same: most of us consistently choose what is unpleasant over what is scary. We will continue down a path of familiar destruction before attempting an unfamiliar alternative. Why? Because fear loves our comfort zone.

Fear paralyzes us from living, thriving, and achieving. It is the voice in our heads that tells us not to hope, not to believe, not to desire anything beyond what we currently know. To stay put because that is where we are safe. Fear is our inner critic, our deepest regrets, Satan, our shadow self, our addictive nature, the Dark Side: whatever we call it, it is a powerful weapon to our psyche. So much so that our society has become afraid of being afraid…and it is destroying our resilience.

We fear what is familiar and unfamiliar; what is present and what is absent. We fear ideas, people, animals, things, life, death, sounds, systems, and even concepts. Take crime, for example. I spent more than 15 years working with philanthropists, community organizers, corporate leaders, government officials, and others on responding to crime and violence in the St. Louis community. I quickly learned that despite our cultural obsession with crime, no one likes thinking about its reality. We dedicate a significant portion of our prime-time and late-night fictional television (as well as much of our 24-hour news cycle) around topics of crime and justice, but the thought of actually experiencing a crime reminds us of how little we can really control. We seek explanations for victimization that imply accountability: "Why do they live in that neighborhood?" "Was she drunk?" "Where were the police?" "Why didn't they lock their doors?" "Well, she should just leave that marriage…." We don't want to acknowledge our powerlessness over some circumstances. This fear—a substantial fear of the unknown and uncontrollable—has paradoxically controlled much of our lives and drives our most counter-productive actions.

When advocates and therapists work with victims to rebuild their lives following crime or violence, they start by assessing what actions, thoughts, or conversations will help the victim reestablish control over their own lives. Those who have experienced violence, war, significant grief, and other sources of trauma know how helpless it feels. We have experienced first-hand what it means to be powerless; to have someone or something control our circumstances. This is the very definition of a victim (a survivor is the person who emerges and heals from these circumstances). It is these experiences that lead us to understand that, while we cannot control everything in our lives, we *can* control the power fear has over us.

When we give in too much to our fears, we become catatonic. We stand still to avoid the potential pain of growth. We fail to achieve even small goals because to do so would risk suffering. We give up, quit, blame, misdirect, excuse, forfeit personal control, or even sue someone else for a circumstance we helped create. We express our feelings online rather than in person out of the fear we may be held personally accountable to others, resulting in the dismissal of others' innate humanity and the destruction of relationships. We create tribes and harass those who think differently just to avoid our fears of conflict, disagreement, or the hard work of critical thinking. We surrender reason in exchange for good feelings. And with each of these moves, fear becomes a whining, energy-consuming bum we can't kick off our mental couch.

We teach children to give in to fear, too. Understandably, we want to protect them against pain or hardship because we love them. So we ignore the inner wisdom that what is difficult or uncomfortable is often what forges us into resilient individuals, capable of navigating the difficulties of life. Instead, we remove any chance of suffering before they can experience it, prioritizing feeling good over disciplined growth by sheltering them from the negative consequences of their actions. We teach them that they are entitled to happiness rather than happiness being a state of mind they experience based on the richness of the life they create. We do this in the hope they will become self-actualized, successful adults. Instead, they are more likely to develop an alarming lack of resilience.

Remember: our baseline responsibility to ourselves is to choose what is best for us. When we shelter ourselves or others from risk, we inadvertently kill innovation, courage, progress, and growth. Is that better than the temporary discomfort or pain experienced from risk? Is the "participation trophy" that spared us from the pain of losing a fair trade for experiencing self-esteem borne of real achievement? Avoidance is an opiate for fear. One that, like a real opiate, grants temporary euphoria but eventually slows, confuses, and depresses us. It is time we trade what makes us comfortable for what makes us resilient.

How Fear Works

When I facilitate new classes or events, one of my favorite ice breakers is to ask, "what's your irrational fear?" We all have them, and they are usually nonsensical and funny. Some of my favorites over the years:

"Seatbelts on planes. Not flying—just the seatbelts."
"That I will crack open an egg and a baby chick will be in there."
"Buttons."
"That I'll wake up one day with amnesia."
"Cotton balls."

"Every time I open a soda can, I wince because I'm sure it's going to spray me in the eye."

"Power windows."

"Poodles. Just…poodles."

This exercise always leaves the room laughing (it's good stuff!). The people who reported these fears are leaders of Fortune 500 companies, business owners, and community leaders. They are among the most credible and dependable people I know, yet they have silly, irrational fears. Why? Because we all do: fear is often an illogical process.

One of my irrational fears is being embarrassed in public. (To be fair, does anyone like it?) One way to overcome fear is to repeatedly subject yourself to the thing you are afraid of. Using this method, one might think I've had enough experience to no longer be afraid of public embarrassment: I've had wardrobe malfunctions onstage, fallen downstairs on live television, given a keynote presentation with a face full of hives, and gotten stuck in a trash can (just to name a few). Ok, let me explain that last one…

A few years ago, I attended a networking event with some key players in my field. Among them was the president of a foundation that had given a significant amount of money to my organization. He stopped to greet me, catching me off-guard as I was taking a large gulp of red wine. I choked mid-sip, and the wine came spilling out my nose (which, it turns out, makes your eyes water like you've been pepper sprayed). My eyes began watering and swelling as I coughed loudly.

Not knowing what to do (and noticing that I was gathering attention), he nervously laughed and said, "well, you don't see that every day!" And walked away. Mortified, I searched for the bathroom to clean myself up. I quickly realized I was not going to be able to salvage my cream-colored shirt from this mess and decided I should leave.

Now, a normal person would've simply walked out the front door. Not me. I opted for the nearest exit, which happened to be at the rear of the building. Just as I neared the door, my eyes started to water furiously again. I wanted on the other side of that door as fast as possible and pushed it open at full speed. My eyes watery and burning, I didn't see the trash can I was running straight into on the other side.

Waist-high, the bin met my speed and teetered me head-first into the trash. Since most of you probably haven't pondered the physics of being stuck upside-down in a trash can, let me help: you can't get out without Herculean strength (I don't have that). Luckily, a catering staff member came out to toss something just seconds after me. Unluckily, I was wearing a skirt.

The nice young man who rescued me earned his angel wings that night. I was on the run, had bloodshot eyes, and red stains on my shirt: he had every reason to mistake me for a serial killer. Instead, he made sure I was okay, graciously smiled, and went back inside. The point of this story? Fear can be funny. It can be ridiculous. And it causes us to do *even worse* things in our effort to escape it.

To understand why fear is such a powerful influence over our lives, it's important to understand how it works. Our fear is useful:

it informs us of potential dangers than could harm us or even kill us. When we perceive a threat, our body signals our flight, fight, or freeze response to act. It is an instantaneous, subconscious, and unavoidable phenomenon built into our DNA to keep us alive. In coordination with our body, our mind kicks into high efficiency and provides us potential shortcuts to avoid pain and threat. Our fight, flight, or freeze response is a lifesaving, effective tool when it's accurate. And it gets us into trouble when it's not. Fortunately, most of us don't experience impending physical danger very often. Unfortunately, we experience emotional danger quite often.

Your brain doesn't always know the difference between an actual threat and a perceived threat (believe me, when I was wine-soaked and being pulled out of a trash can I was sure I was going to *actually* die of embarrassment!). You may feel a similar response to an impending car accident as you do to the boss calling you into her office. One could result in actual death, but your brain also recognizes the danger of an emotional death and stands guard on your behalf. Our brains spend a great deal of time firing signals that difficult emotions or unknown circumstances are evidence that something is about to go terribly wrong and, if we're not careful, could even kill us. It doesn't know—and therefore doesn't tell us—that our system is overreacting to the stimulus.

Being rejected by someone we love shouldn't feel the same as pulling a muscle in our chest, but it does. Because our emotions protect us from harm the same way our bodies do. Our fight, flight, or freeze response is like our minds searching a medical diagnosis website: sometimes it saves our lives, other times it takes a single symptom and fills our head with a hundred possible maladies we will never experience.

For those who suffer anxiety, the fight, flight, or freeze phenomenon is on overdrive. Even small changes in the environment can feel like significant, impending threats. Science has come a long way in helping us understand and address clinical anxiety, providing pharmaceutical and therapeutic interventions that successfully curb anxiety's grip on our wellness. These medical and psychological tools can make tremendous difference in the daily function of those who suffer from anxiety, and they should be utilized without shame. That said, it is critical to remember that these interventions are only *part* of the solution. It is also up to us to cognitively dismantle our fears and use them to our advantage: to move beyond our comfort zone. Instead of working exhaustedly to build safe walls around our lives to avoid anything that triggers pain, disappointment, regret, failure, suffering, or loss, *what if we put that energy into using fear to our advantage?* If we evaluate our fear for the information it is providing us—the growth it may be pointing us toward—we have an opportunity to gain insight and personal development from fear.

Embracing the Resistance

Many years ago, I served as the Executive Director of a youth symphony. Though I knew music generally, I had very little experience with the wide variety of instruments represented in an orchestra, so I loved when the students stopped by for practice sessions. I would pause my work and watch, learning more about how each instrument told its story.

One afternoon, a young violinist came by the office to meet with his conductor. He was an accomplished musician, his fingers quickly and easily peppering the neck of his violin. He practiced a bit, made some adjustments, and practiced some more.

I love the violin—it's one of my favorite instruments. I find it capable of a wide range of emotions, sounding vibrant, melancholy, anxious, angry, or peaceful. The young man played the same few bars over and over, listening for perfection. He was getting increasingly frustrated, though I wasn't sure what he was aiming for. The conductor stopped him and said, "you want it to be easy. You need more resistance. Resistance creates the most beautiful music."

Resistance creates the most beautiful music. I knew he was speaking technically, but I heard it metaphorically. Life's most beautiful music is never created in the easiest moments; it's forged during, or after, tremendous resistance. The student placed his bow and, with a little more resistance, began to play. Sure enough, the sound changed noticeably, like a sigh moving to a groan.

Resilient people embrace resistance. They don't waste time on the fear or discomfort that tension and resistance bring. They know pushing through their challenges will create the most beautiful music. Victory is reserved for those who use resistance to their advantage.

When I ask my clients what they want more of in their lives, I get a variety of answers including growth, success, excitement, adventure, contentment, and happiness. The problem is, you won't find any of those where you are comfortable. Comfortable is a reflection of what is, not of what can be. To experience something different, you must *do* something different. **The radical truth is everything you crave lies just beyond your comfort zone.**

I assert this statement to individuals I work with. We then spend time outlining what their fears are, what experience (or lack of experience) may have created them, which fears are legitimate (based on a real or likely threat), and what happiness they believe might be discovered if they moved past their fears. I challenge them to discover whether fear is what stops them or what pushes them to be better than they imagined they could be.

Before we talk about using fear to our advantage, we talk about the many forms it can take and the ways it can steal our greatest moments. I ask clients what they think holds them back from what they want more of in their lives. For example, a fear of learning new skills—or perhaps the fear of failing at those skills—keeps us from growing into a more capable person. A fear of giving up control of minor and unimportant details keeps us from experiencing more peace. A fear of failure leads to procrastination and sometimes, ironically, eventual failure rather than the success we crave. And so on until, despite how desperately we may want something to be different, we find ourselves complacent because we refuse to leave our comfort zone.

One of the most common fears I hear during this exercise is the fear of love: as a partner, as a parent, as a child, as a friend. In whatever way love finds us, we can be paralyzed by its power (and even more so by its loss). I know many beautiful, amazing people who have so much to give to friends or a partner but hide it behind a fear of rejection, abandonment, failure, or loss.

Experiencing unconditional love is life-changing…as is its loss, so it's understandable why we equally seek and avoid it.

Perhaps worst among the love-avoidance reasons I have heard is the assertion that we are simply *not lovable*. This is fear turned malevolence, robbing us of the purest joy life has to offer us. "I'm unlovable" is an excuse. It is a self-fulfilling prophecy found at the intersection of self-pity and emotional laziness. "I'm unlovable" and "I'm not good enough" lead us to push others away in punishment for crimes not yet committed, while we escape into an imperme-able psychological cocoon: a comfort zone of catastrophic propor-tion. This cocoon is an illusion. We don't emerge a better version of ourselves. Instead, we wither and stagnate inside while forcing others to stand outside, missing out on the greatest gift we can give or receive.

Allowing others to love us is hard. It requires us to accept our own raw, messy humanity and trust another will accept it as well. It means acknowledging our imperfections, admiring our strengths, and inviting another pass judgment on our greatest vulnerabilities. Allowing love, especially self-love, into our lives requires immense courage: exactly the kind of courage that makes a person resilient.

Resilient people allow themselves to be loved for all they are (and are not). They do not allow heartbreak to discourage them from future love. They understand that the value of love is worth the courage it requires. *They know that every fear they overcome makes them a better person and brings them closer to the life they want.*

When you were a child, what were you afraid of? Not fitting in with other kids? Getting in trouble with your parents? Failing academically so that you might not get into college and achieve your career goals? All of these were great motivators for success. You stretched your comfort level to learn new things, tolerate different personalities, and identify the uniqueness in others so you'd fit in. To avoid being grounded, you behaved in obedient ways that eventually shaped you into a conscientious adult. You studied hard to procure the future you wanted. Sometimes it was painful, but it always taught you something valuable.

As an adult, you have a much better understanding of the power of your fears. Do they hold you back, or catapult you to your goals? When was the last time you did something difficult just for the sake of accomplishment? Do you stand up for yourself when the stakes are high? Have you walked away from that toxic relationship? Doing what is best for us is not taking the easy path. It's not meant to be easy. Resistance is there to push us to the next level.

If we stay in our comfort zones we wither and eventually die: metaphorically, emotionally, and even sometimes literally. Resistance, in the form of life's challenges, is necessary for our survival. Think of childbirth: it is one of the most violent experiences our bodies can go through, yet the only way to begin the miracle of life. It is only under the most intense pressure that diamonds are created, making them precious and beautiful. Only in darkness do seeds burst open into the food that gives us life. In fact, our entire universe exists only because extreme tension and resistance created it. The discomfort of resistance is a gift that brings necessary growth and development. The challenge lies in becoming comfortable with—and even welcoming—that resistance.

Conquering Your Fears

To conquer our fears requires a shift in mindset. We must see fear as a necessary adversary and challenges as our guides. The resilient person—the warrior, if you will—is called upon to consult their fears and use them as tools for success. At its worst, fear is a liar. At its best, it is a powerful catalyst for powerful growth. For example, identifying your fear of rejection gives you valuable information about what you believe about being alone, or about your self-worth. Identifying your fear of poverty provides information about what you believe about money and its role in your happiness.

Your fears are constantly giving you information and advice and, once you have it, you can choose what you will do with it: dismiss it because you recognize it as a meritless emotional or primordial response, or act on it in life-changing ways because you recognize it as wisdom. Either way, it's calling on you to *deal with it*.

If you fail to deal with your fear, your mind will respond in ways that feel anxious or depressed. Anxiety occurs when you fail to eliminate a fear, depression when you refuse to act on what you know it is teaching you. Those who develop lifestyles of avoidance rank among the unhappiest in the world. In fact, studies show that countries where people value experiences over material goods are the happiest. This is not by accident: experiences take us out of our comfort zone and challenge us to live fully.

When people are interviewed at the end of their lives, one of their most common regrets is not having lived their fullest life by taking advantage of all the opportunities they had available to them. They feared what others might think, what others wanted from them, or doubted their own abilities and therefore stayed in their comfort zones. Perhaps our only fear should be ending our lives without having overcome our fears! Because the true cost of fear is that we forfeit our authentic happiness and deepest growth.

If your life is not going the way you want, discover what fears are holding you back. Sure, circumstances can thwart us, but more often we (and we alone) are the reason for our lack of progress. We have much more control than we think. But we wait, quit, dismiss, avoid, blame, sleep, procrastinate, wallow, sacrifice, pivot, and bury just to avoid acting. Think about how much energy, time, and work it takes to avoid taking right action! What fears can you face head-on to save yourself from a life of wasted time and opportunities? What can you do right now to eliminate what isn't important and focus on what is?

EXERCISE: SO WHAT? THEN WHAT?

When I or someone I know is trapped in the loop of fear, I ask the questions, "So what? Then what?" This is my way of getting to the root of what is really at stake. Let's say I don't get the job I applied for. *So what?* It's not the only job I'll ever be rejected for, and it's not the only opportunity out there. *Then what?* I will continue to apply for other jobs because clearly this was not the opportunity meant for me.

It sounds easier than it is, but if you can master this process, it will help you get out of the emotional side of fear and into its more practical application. Which is where we want to be because very few things are life-or-death (despite our mind's ability to make us feel otherwise).

Try the following exercise to learn this process for yourself. Think about an area of your life that isn't going the way you want it to, something you may be procrastinating on or avoiding altogether. Let's say, for example, you have been wanting to ask for a raise for several months but find yourself holding back. Ask yourself the following questions:

1. What are my beliefs about this subject? *(In this case, asking for a merit raise)*
   Examples:
   - *I believe that asking for more money may indicate selfishness, and I don't want to be a selfish person.*
   - *I believe wanting money, or being rich, is bad.*
   - *Conceited people ask for raises.*

2. What fears or limiting beliefs are holding me back?
   Examples:
   - *I may be turned down (and I fear rejection).*
   - *I'm afraid I don't really deserve a raise.*
   - *I will be seen as materialistic.*

3. If any of these fears are true, so what? Then what?
   Examples:
   - *I may be turned down for the raise, but I will live. I'm certainly not the first person to ask for more money and not receive it—it happens every day!*
   - *I know I deserve the raise because I have outlined my case for it: I have the experience, it has been two years since*

my last raise, and I have met or exceeded all my perfor-mance objectives.

- *I will be seen as materialistic, but not by those who know me well, and they are who really matter.*

As you can see, taking the time to walk through a fear can be an important step in overcoming it. Most of our fears are emotional reactions that need to be met with logical prowess. Working through these steps helps us understand why we have the fear and develop a plan for dealing with its potential consequences. Most of us, when armed with a plan, find it much easier to dismiss fear.

The Source of Fear

Being resilient relies heavily on identifying the sources of your fears so you can overcome them. Fear requires us to identify its lies, grapple with its truths, and conquer it until it catapults us into a better version of ourselves. This growth is not always a linear or easy process, because our minds are inherently complicated and messy. Our minds operate from a lifetime of experiences and false notions that leave us equally afraid of the known and unknown. Some of our fears are so common they are experienced by nearly everyone, others are as unique as we are. But whatever we fear, getting to the root cause is the catalyst for eliminating it.

Humans have so many fears that entire careers are dedicated to studying them. In researching this book, I delved into dozens of studies that gauged our top fears. The results vary widely, but most lists were topped off by fear of change, illness, loss of a loved one, death, social unrest and war, phobias (spiders, the dark, etc.), and—you guessed it—public speaking.

That last one may be surprising…except to those who are afraid of public speaking! Despite being a theater major in college, I was absolutely terrified of public speaking. I put off Speech 101 until my final semester, avoiding it until graduating depended upon it. My fear was so great that, though I was on track to graduate Magna Cum Laude, I only hoped for a strong C in the class. I started off the semester as I expected: I stuttered my way through the beginning of each speech and ended it exhausted and nauseated.

A few weeks in, the professor pulled me aside and accused me of using my fear of speaking as an excuse for my lack of preparation. I couldn't blame her; it didn't make sense that I was accustomed to performing in front of thousands of people but couldn't manage a simple speech in front of thirty classmates! I showed her my notes to convince her that I was truly prepared each time. I worked with classmates who excelled at speaking to discover their secret. Nothing seemed to work.

Finally, I sought the advice of the campus therapist. I had never been to a therapist: this was during a time when it was still somewhat taboo to seek mental health services (I am thankful this is no longer the case). But it was such a strange, paradoxical phenomenon for *me*—the girl who could act or sing confidently in front of anyone—that I thought I must be really "off" and in need of professional help.

Through therapy I learned something important about myself: I had a deep fear of people knowing the "real" me. On stage, I presented a character; if you didn't like her, that was ok—she wasn't me, anyway! But to put my real ideas and thoughts out there, and to have to state those with everyone staring at me, felt incredibly raw and vulnerable. What if they didn't agree with my points? What if I made a fool of myself? *What if they thought I was stupid?* We explored what experiences led to this fear and how I could work around it. To her credit, she was able to convince me I'd be okay even *if* all these things occurred (and that they were not very likely to). By the end of the semester, I made a (somewhat hesitant) peace with public speaking and received a B in the class. More importantly, I learned my first valuable lesson about the power and irrationality of our fears.

Now, I absolutely love public speaking and seek any opportunity to do it. I find it exhilarating to connect with an audience, sharing information that might help others overcome a difficulty or learn something new. I think often about my former fear of it because it reminds me how truly powerful and paralyzing our fears can be.

EXERCISE: THE SPARK TOOL®

Several years ago, I developed the SPARK Tool to help my clients identify and overcome the fears that hold themselves and their teams back. Think of a fear that you are struggling with, and apply this process:

1. **SEEK** the purpose of your fear. Identify the underlying source of the fear: did a specific incident or threat occur? Is there a value or belief that has been violated? Does this fear have credibility, or is it an emotional response that

may not be based in fact? What *information* is this fear
providing me?

2. **PAUSE.** Breathe through the fear for at least 2 minutes,
   releasing its power over your body. Now ask yourself: will
   I still be afraid of this an hour from now? How about a
   day? What does that tell you about the fear's validity?

3. **ACT.** If the fear is legitimate, it is calling you to act. What
   is your plan? How will you address and overcome the
   fear? Be specific and realistic—the better the plan for
   success, the faster you will eliminate the impact of this
   fear.

4. **REVIEW.** Think of the worst-case scenario of this fear.
   Determine how you will be okay even if this happens.
   Now visualize the outcome. What's the best that could
   happen? Visualize exactly that happening. Be specific and
   visualize it multiple times.

5. **KEEP it up.** The best way to overcome a fear is to face
   it and face it repeatedly if necessary. If directly experiencing your fear is not safe or possible, keep reviewing
   the mental portions of this process until the fear feels
   manageable.

We're Not Alone

Fear, like many emotions, is contagious. Studies show that, just
like our individual primordial responses to fear, we have "group-
think" primordial responses to fear (called "mass hysteria"). Our
individual fear becomes *more powerful* when driven by this group

response. History provides us several sad or fascinating examples of the effects of this kind of fear, including the Salem Witch Trials, War of the Worlds radio broadcast, and strange phenomenon like laughing epidemics. While many incidents of mass hysteria are rooted in valid and logical fears, just as many are not. The effects of mass hysteria are widespread and more dangerous than fear at an individual level.

Have you ever heard a rumor at work that there are about to be layoffs? Think about how people reacted: some became nervous, others angry, still others catatonic. Whether the rumor was based in fact or not, it was widely known in a short time. Some companies have experience mass resignations based on a false rumor. I know of one company whose employees stole supplies and small electronics after hearing a false rumor not of layoffs, but of reduced bonuses!

The digital age has made mass hysteria a thriving business. Our comfort zones encompass the information we want to believe, that agrees with our world view, despite whether it's true. Getting out of our comfort zone requires us to question, search, and double-check what we hear and learn. It takes diligence and cognitive effort. Rumors spread quickly through social media, and, whether true or not, cause widespread division, animosity, and even violence. It is incumbent upon each of us to challenge our sources, dig deeper for information, and second-guess what we hear until we have better information. No source of information is safe from imperfection, so we must hold ourselves to a high expectation of verification. Before sharing, posting, or commenting, find out if the story is true. Learn *both* sides of the story. Before complaining to a colleague about a new company policy, make sure you understand if or why it's being created. The point is, we each play a role in perpetrating—or halting—a significant amount of shared fear in our communities.

The saddest part of negotiating with fear is our pervasive belief that it is so much more powerful than it actually is. Fear convinces us it has the upper hand in every scenario. When we can dismiss it or use it to our advantage, we win.

Resilience requires us to face our fears head-on, narrowing them down by their usefulness. We are required to learn from our fear, utilizing it repeatedly until we learn the lesson and make the growth. Fear will continue to tap our shoulder until we conquer or eliminate it. That's its job. If we can push beyond our comfort zone and embrace the tension fear creates, we will find the richness and contentment life is calling us to experience.

A Note on Trauma

In addition to the natural fears we all possess, there are circumstances and experiences that create trauma within us. This is a new and different type of fear marked by a specific set of emotional and physiological responses and is a reaction to a specific type of extreme event. While you can overcome trauma, it is not as easy as mitigating everyday fears. We experience trauma in three forms: acute (a single incident), chronic (several incidents of a similar kind), or complex (multiple incidents of varying kinds over time). Whatever type of trauma a person experiences, it is painful, often debilitating, and can feel uncontrollable. Some, but not all, trauma becomes Post-Traumatic Stress Disorder (PTSD), which is different from but is as equally or more disruptive than trauma. Both trauma and PTSD are widely misunderstood by the public, so while this book does not address these directly, I highly encourage you to learn more about them. The better informed we are about mental health, the better we can serve ourselves and others if needed.

The fear responses I discuss in this chapter and throughout this book are not trauma specific. While some of the same strategies apply, overcoming true traumatic responses requires a different and more intensive approach to healing. If you or someone you know is experiencing the symptoms of trauma (difficulty functioning, unpredictable emotions, flashbacks, strained relationships, intrusive thoughts,s or hyper-vigilance, just to name a few), please refer them to a mental health professional. While people can make great strides addressing their own trauma, professional help is the best way to ensure lasting healing from a traumatic event.

For Reflection

Answer the following questions alone or with a group:

1. What fears are holding you back?
   - *How would it feel if you overcame these fears to achieve your goals?*
   - *Which feels better to imagine: your comfort zone, or the achievement?*
2. What does resilience look like to you? How are your fears keeping you from living resiliently?
3. Name a specific fear that is keeping you from achieving a desired goal or outcome. Now:
   - *Identify how you will increase your exposure to the source of this fear to develop tolerance of it (i.e., scheduling speaking opportunities to become more comfortable with public speaking).*
   - *Identify at least one way you can mitigate or eliminate the fear through risk management, skill building, or better thinking.*
4. What is your irrational fear? How might you minimize or overcome it?
5. Identify a fear and write down the information it is providing you about yourself, your beliefs, or your choices.

PRINCIPLE TWO:

SELF-AWARENESS IS YOUR SUPERPOWER

To know thyself is the beginning of wisdom.

—Socrates

Who Are You?

"Who are you?"

"Julie," I answered. He was an aging man, but had he forgotten my name that quickly? He smiled, and asked again, "No, who *are* you?"

The question confused and irritated me. He stood with his hands in his pockets and watched me haul water across the yard. Tired from unforgiving Missouri August heat, I just wanted to finish the job I had come to do, which today entailed caring for dogs in a large backyard kennel.

Dr. Nelson's house was one of my favorite places to visit in my college years. He and his wife had curated a comfortable and eccentric house filled with antiques and strange knickknacks from all over the world. I loved hearing about each item or book—its story, purpose, or origin. A theology professor and minister, he told meaningful and esoteric stories about his travels and experiences. Their house piqued my inquisitive nature.

I was occasionally paid a nominal fee (a fortune to a college student) to help them with routine household tasks. I suspected then—and am sure now—these odd jobs were a way for him to keep an eye on a sensitive student struggling to find her way.

"Who am I? I'm Julie. I don't know what else," I answered.

"Then you're going to have a rough go of it, dear," he said, chuckling as he walked inside.

A few short years later, as I was recovering from my assault, I was unsure how—or if—I would function again. I was broken, beaten, and ashamed. My understanding of the world had been irreparably altered. Impatient with my inability to restore myself mentally or physically, I quit my job and moved back home to be near family…which inadvertently made me feel like more of a failure. Meanwhile, the trauma of what had happened consumed my thoughts day and night, impenetrable to logic or sympathy.

On a particularly rough afternoon, I remembered this conversation with Dr. Nelson. He had since passed away, leaving a Merlin-sized hole in my life. I missed how he challenged me to think deeply and carefully about the responsibilities of being human; to understand how easily, if we were not vigilant, we could slide between the best and worst of our nature (and that each of us is inherently capable of both). Would I be able to hold onto my better self when surrounded by such pain and hopelessness?

"Who *are* you?" I heard him ask again. This time I understood. My job in this moment was to know *everything* I could about myself. My life, my wellbeing, depended on understanding how I was going to get through this experience. *What was I made of?* I needed to understand my personality, my character, my values, my abilities, my weaknesses, and what I held in my psychological reserves for life's stormy days. Was I the person who would give up, or the person who would heal? Was it my nature to find purpose in this experience, or to harbor resentment for the rest of my life? Was I capable or incapable of resilience? What would healing look like for me, and what was I willing to invest of my body and spirit to achieve it? What did I believe about human nature and the phenomenon of forgiveness? *Who was I?*

I was no more able to answer that question than I had been when Dr. Nelson posed it five years earlier. But I figured if I couldn't describe who I was, I could at least determine who I *wanted* to be. I got up from the couch and wrote two columns on a page, titling them "personal best" and "personal worst." I wanted to know the best- and worst-case scenarios of who I would be going forward. Who did I want to be after this experience? Who did I *need* to be to save myself?

In the "worst-case scenario" column I listed things like "angry and terrified," "in physical or emotional pain," "bitter and unforgiving," and "existing without friends or love." In the "best-case scenario" column I wrote "able to overcome grief," "an end to hopelessness," and "great relationships with family, friends, and boyfriend." I could see what my hopes were for myself. I looked at this list often, reminding myself of what I needed to do. I could determine which behaviors would lead me to the best outcomes, and which thoughts embraced who I wanted to be. This certainly wasn't the entirety of my path to healing—that included time, a loving family, and a good therapist— but it was an important first step.

I have carried this practice forward and shared it with others to help them identify both who they are and who they are becoming. When faced with adversity, we discover hidden talents and characteristics we didn't know we possessed. More importantly, we have an opportunity to determine which characteristics we *want* to possess. It's the magic of every challenge we face.

Whether it's a personal or professional challenge, what reserves do you pull from? Who are you in the face of frustration, grief, or difficulties? What leads you to behave in the ways you do, and what experiences build your thoughts? Some of this you can answer now, some of it you can imagine based on your knowledge of self, but much of it waits for the right introduction: the challenge or difficulty that allows you to discover the answer, to discover who you really are.

When the Emperor is Naked

In Hans Christian Andersen's classic tale, *The Emperor Has New Clothes*, we learn of an emperor so obsessed with fine clothing that swindlers are able to convince him he looks splendidly clad…even when he is embarrassingly naked. His noblemen (and later the community) go along with this idea, worried it's their own perception that is off. They don't want to see reality, don't want to be the one to criticize, or don't want to be the lone voice speaking truth. Eventually the truth comes out and everyone, to their relief, can agree he is indeed naked.

The story is a cautionary tale of going along with lies even when truth is apparent, but I always wondered what was going on in the emperor's mind. Why wasn't he *sure* he was naked? What level of vanity made him fall prey to the swindlers' assertion that he looked great? And what kind of influence did he have that could make his noblemen awkwardly pretend to dress him in refined nothingness?

I think of this parable often when I witness someone who lacks self-awareness. For me, the more important point of this story is that the emperor should have known himself well enough to recognize he was being fooled from the beginning. He should've possessed enough humility to assume that he could be duped, and therefore double-check his assumptions. And he should've empowered his noblemen to know they are safe to speak up when something seems off. While we are all guilty of allowing others to define us from time to time, he flagrantly ignored the whispers of townspeople who were acknowledging he was naked. Instead, he continued to strut proudly in his imaginary refinery. **How often do we continue to strut, oblivious to our naked behavior?**

Many of the individuals I have coached over the years fail to understand the importance of **observable behavior** in the self-awareness process. What is observable is real: when the emperor didn't see clothing on his body, he should've known he was naked! Instead, some fall prey to the ego, defining who they are by who they wish they are (often based on an ideal set forth by others). When challenged, they are unable to identify behaviors that support this idea. For example, "I'm a generous person" is an incorrect perception of self if there are no acts of generosity that can be remembered, witnessed, or identified. To be a generous person we must act generously. We must think generously. And we must know what our motivation is for wanting to be seen as a generous person.

Resilient people know themselves. Their self-perception matches their behavior, and their perception of others is rooted in others' observable behaviors. Thus, others' feedback doesn't often surprise a resilient person. While someone else's perception of us certainly isn't always true or reliable, we should know ourselves well enough not to be surprised by the impression we leave.

When there is a gap between how we see our behavior and how others see it (given we trust the other person's perception), it is usually for one of two reasons: (1) our intention and behavior are misaligned or (2) we are not being fully honest with ourselves about who we are.

When our intention is misaligned with our behavior, you'll notice you feel frustrated and misunderstood. You seek to reassure yourself: "but I am this kind of person," "but I do care about…," or "but my intent was…." You can identify a real quality or emotion within yourself, but perhaps not how you actively exhibit it. This problem is usually the result of being busy, distracted, because of differences in communication, or because we are uncomfortable expressing certain feelings. A good example of this is expressing gratitude: we often appreciate the efforts of others but, in the day-to-day hum of life, forget to specifically express it. With better attention and trustworthy feedback, it's easy to identify what you did (or didn't) do to set the right impression and make behavioral adjustments to improve.

Lacking honesty with ourselves, however, is trickier. It requires a level of vulnerability and self-inspection that can be uncomfortable. We "try on" other personas and wonder why they don't fit. We create entire digital lives that are branded and curated to make ourselves appear the way we want others to see us, then wonder why we feel isolated and misunderstood. We work harder at convincing ourselves that we are who others want us to be than we work at optimizing our own gifts. And if we're not careful, it leads us straight into the shackles of hypocrisy.

When we try to be something we are not, behave in ways that do not uphold our inherent values, or create standoffs between our words and actions, we enter the territory of hypocrisy. And if we're really in deep, we don't even realize we are acting in absolute contrast to our stated beliefs and values. This contrast makes trust between us and others an impossibility. Simply put, hypocrisy is born in the void of self-awareness.

There's an adage I have used in my leadership training for years: **the amount of space between what you say you will do and what you do is equal to the amount of distrust experienced.** If you say you will have a critical report to your boss by 5pm and you deliver it at 5:15pm, there is likely only a small or inconsequential dip in trust. If you say, however, that you will have the report to your boss by 5pm, do not turn it in, and leave for a 2-week vacation, you have created a chasm of distrust. We often, without knowledge or intent, create these chasms. It is up to us to be aware when we create them and do what we can to remedy them before they damage the underlying relationship. To build and maintain trust, we must do what we say what we will do and veer away from the dangers of hypocrisy.

In speaking with employees across a variety of sectors, I have learned hypocritical practices create distrust with increasing and troubling frequency. Administrators may talk a great game about employee wellness while increasing hours and decreasing pay or benefits. Leaders boast their commitment to autonomy and flexibility while micromanaging their staff. Companies lament that they are losing quality employees while doing little to incentivize or praise good performance. At best these contradictions create confusion, and at worst, a disheartening lack of trust.

In a 2021 study conducted by Reins Institute, 41% of employers surveyed reported they have cut retirement parties, recognition ceremonies, and/or most incentive gifts in recent years. The result? Employees stated they believe loyalty to their company (as defined by 10 or more years of service), as well as showing increased effort and initiative in the workplace, will not have a meaningful personal result. The practice of cutting recognition programs demoralized employees at a time when companies were desperate to retain good talent. Yet these companies were, in large part, unaware of the double-standard they had created between their stated desires and observable actions.

Hypocrisy also infects our societal institutions. For example, social media influencers lecture the public on "body positivity" and "embracing our true selves" while significantly altering their appearance with software and filters. Local governments boast a dedication to safety and education while pulling money and resources from both. And, too often, companies clamor to publicly assert their social impact statements—their dedication to making the world a better place through equity, inclusion, and environmental responsibility—while creating the very problems they commit to solving.

People are smart, and they are intuitive. When hypocrisy rears its ugly head, they notice, and they begin distrusting the systems in which they work and live. If we want to be resilient, and raise resilient children, we must be able to rely on trustworthy relationships. **The more self-aware humanity is, the more trust it will sow.** It is time we embrace self-reflection, eliminate any gaps between what we say we will do and what we observably do, and reestablish trust in our relationships, companies, and communities.

Defined by Others

Have you ever changed your style, hobbies, or behavior for a person you're romantically interested in, to meet family expectations, or to fit in with friends? Most of us have. And most of us discovered how disastrous it can be! Eventually the depression of living a false identity catches up with us. Our mission as warriors of resilience is not to create a false persona, allow others to define who we are, or blame others for how we behave. **Our mission requires us to fiercely evaluate who we are and fine-tune that person into who we are meant to be.**

I remember a time early in my career when I believed I had identified the "right" behaviors for professionalism. Somewhere along the way I had come to believe that women who are taken seriously must behave seriously. Naturally bubbly, humorous, and light-hearted, this was difficult for me.

I watched leaders who seemed to be taken seriously and tried to emulate their behaviors. I wanted to appear focused and driven, so I placed a high level of importance on everything, including things that didn't deserve it. I worked more hours than necessary, held back any engagement with others I thought would be perceived as frivolous, and came dangerously close to micromanaging. Unsurprisingly, I received feedback that included adjectives like, "inflexible," "tightly-wound," and even "stuck up" (ouch). What astounds me still today was that I was surprised by this feedback— of course I came across that way! If we act in ways that are counterintuitive to our natural strengths, we are likely to fail. I had to realize my strength as a fun, inspiring leader and find environments that supported those qualities, rather than try to fit into environments that require me to be someone else.

The closer we are to honestly knowing and accepting ourselves, the better we succeed even when we are required to stretch beyond our intuitive nature. We are most successful when we operate with few-to-no gaps between how we see ourselves and how others perceive us.

EXERCISE: HOW ARE YOU VIEWED?

If you find you are frequently confused or surprised by feedback you receive from those you trust, you have a great opportunity to observe and learn about your own behavior. Using the following steps, ask a trusted source to help you identify areas for growth:

1. Identify a quality you would like to embody but are unsure if others perceive you this way. (For example, you might say, I want to be seen as an encouraging person.)

2. Evaluate yourself for how well you think you embody your chosen quality. Is this quality a natural strength or a weakness for you? More importantly: why do you want to be seen this way (i.e., why does being "encouraging" matter to you)?

3. Ask a trusted source (friend, partner, colleague, etc.) for a baseline assessment. Start by acknowledging you are working on this quality and would appreciate honest feedback. This could mean asking something as direct as, "generally speaking, do you believe I am a _____ person?" or you can ask for feedback on specific circumstances.

4. Ask the person the following:

    a. What does [desired quality] look like to you? In other words, how would you know if I am exhibiting this quality?

    b. Do I communicate this quality in words or actions? Can you name any examples?

    c. What would you like me to do to better demonstrate that I am [desired quality]?

The good thing about this exercise is that it nearly always creates change. Either we identify improved ways to demonstrate a desired quality through behavior, or we realize we are not really committed to demonstrating the behavior to begin with (such as I learned in my "serious" phase).

Thought + Behavior = Reality

There is a movement afoot that promotes the role of thought in creating our reality. Books on manifestation, abundance, and even some quantum physics theories suggest we can create a desired outcome through an arrangement of specific thoughts. While I do not deny the role of thought in creating a specific outcome (particularly the role of positive thinking), I find thought alone to be a simplistic explanation of how this phenomenon works. It leaves out the most important part: our active role in creating the life, organization, or community we want.

What we do creates who we are. Do you want to lose weight? You can want it desperately, you can think about it constantly, you can mediate and pray on it, but unless you actively engage in practices that result in weight loss (dieting, exercising, adhering to medical advice, etc.), you are not a person who is losing weight. If you want to be rich, but do not do anything to make money, it is very unlikely you will suddenly become rich (even in the rare case of winning the lottery, you still must take the action of going to a store and buying the ticket!). Who we want to be, and who we think we are, are only a small part of our selves. Our behaviors are the true, observable indicators of who we are.

Those who are self-aware have mastered an understanding of two key factors: 1) what we think (including our emotions), and 2) how those thoughts manifest into actions (what we do). Our thoughts and actions tell us what is important to us, what we are committed to, and perhaps most importantly, what fears or beliefs are holding us back. If we understand the origin of our thoughts and behaviors, we can pick up critical clues to understanding each of these components.

Self-awareness can be like trying to see your own back: it's difficult unless you consciously and creatively seek ways to view it. If I asked you to try, you'd use a mirror, right? But how can you be sure your mirror isn't distorted, providing a fun-house view of yourself? That's why facts are critical to developing self-awareness. They are measurable, sensory, observable, and leave little room for distortion. The better we observe our own actions, thoughts, and behaviors, the better we become at identifying who we are—and how we will master life's greatest challenges.

What We Think: Developing Perspective

We function in our world from one perspective: our own. The better we know ourselves, the better we are at adapting to the world around us. This is because self-knowledge allows us to para-doxically see how we differ from others, what we might learn from these differences, and how we fit into our world. If we are self-aware—if we know what drives our behaviors and thoughts and how those things affect others—we are capable of a rich and well-developed perspective. If we lack self-awareness, our perspective is rigid and unforgiving, creating dimensionless ideas that result in a troubled and incorrect view of the world.

Our personal perspective is created by our upbringing, family structure, emotions, values, religion, neurological and physical state, education, race and ethnicity, gender, personal experiences, genetic makeup, learned behaviors, and much, much more. It is both reliable and unreliable. And what is most important about our perspective is that it informs our understanding of the truth. Our perspective is activated as soon as we experience any stimuli (real or imagined). It is grounded in three experiences: **learned, witnessed, and imagined**. To hone our perspective to be reflec-tive of reality, we must lean on what we can observe. In the case of self-awareness, this is our behavior.

Our **learned experiences** are how we have directly experi-enced the circumstances, thoughts, and emotions of life. It is the closest we can get to reality. Direct experience provides thoughts and emotions that become the catalyst for our behaviors. A contin-uous loop is created that provides context for the truth: what we experience informs our thoughts, our thoughts create our behav-iors, our behaviors shape our experiences, and on it goes.

Let's say you were recently fired from your job. You would know first-hand the feelings of panic, shame, and grief that often follow being fired. You have emotional, physical, and even cellular memory of this experience. You might also have greater sympathy for someone else experiencing being fired or be more adept to sensitively inform someone that they are being fired. Directly learned experience, though sometimes painful because it is first-person, is our most reliable source of information for developing perspective because it is real and comprehensive. If you've ever been fired, you know first-hand how difficult it is (and however great the lessons it provided, you probably never want to be fired again).

Maybe you haven't personally been fired, but your parent was when you were a child. This is your second most powerful creator of perspective: **the witness**. You experience life by observing someone else's emotional response, stated thoughts, or behaviors regarding an experience, which informs you of what it means to you. If your parent handled being fired with optimism, you are more likely to see being fired for the opportunity it may provide versus feeling only despair. If the firing led to the loss of your home or even your parent's marriage, however, you are likely to view being fired as one of the worst things that can happen to you. You have less control over what you learn from others' experiences, making them a less reliable source to develop perspective. But that doesn't mitigate the importance of learning from others: much of what we understand about the world (and the right choices for us) comes from what we learn from others' triumphs and failures. In fact, studies show that highly intelligent people often learn more from witnessing others' experiences than having to experience it directly. It is a built-in shortcut for the observer to avoid painful consequences while gaining valuable information.

But now let's imagine you've never been fired, nor has anyone you know. What will you think about this experience? You may have no way of understanding why it would be difficult, what happens when someone is fired, or how one might feel after being fired. You are now left with two choices: to **imagine** the experience (empathy) or ignore it (elimination). In order to successfully navigate our relationships, we most often choose empathy.

Empathy and Self-awareness

Empathy is getting a lot of attention these days, and rightfully so: it is how we create internal context to help us relate to those who have experienced something we have little or no point of reference for. Empathy allows us to imagine how we would handle challenges we do not have direct or learned experience with. The next step, self-awareness, allows us to imagine how our perception of these challenges may differ from how others experience them. Self-aware people are intimately in touch with their emotions, tendencies, motivations, and capabilities, providing a richer imagination of how others may navigate their experiences.

For example, most of us do not have to have a diagnosis of cancer (or even know someone who has) to understand why it would be incredibly difficult. Our empathy allows us to imagine this hardship, sometimes even eliciting palpable anxiety or grief. The self-aware person can imagine this at a deeper level, considering how someone else might experience it differently because they are equipped with different strengths, perspectives, and circumstances. Empathy is a uniquely human gift that provides relationship to others. It comes more easily for some people, but it is possible to be developed by all. And it should be developed and encouraged because it helps us create the final piece of our perspective: discerning facts from the unknown.

Like a fingerprint, your experiences (direct, witnessed, or those discerned from empathy) culminate over time into your unique, personal perspective. All the information you've gathered, your actions, your feelings, and your unique attributes have given you a one-of-a-kind view of the world unlike anyone else's. Our mind places all this information into categories of "good," "neutral," or "bad" to navigate our world. This process is natural, and necessary for our safety and well-being. It informs how successfully we relate to others. But problems arise when our perspective is the result of miscategorized information.

When Our Perspective is Wrong

Our perspective is off when it is not grounded in something observable, or if we have misunderstood what we observed. How we think is a reaction to both the observable, fact-based lessons in our lives but also our fears, emotions, and misunderstandings we've experienced, or because of misinformation. Our thoughts reflect both our real and imaginary joys and sorrows, making fact-finding the most important goal of self-awareness.

Facts help us avoid creating inaccurate context because they are simple: what happened, what was said, what was done, what could be seen, heard, or felt. **Facts are not positive or negative**

until we assign these attributes. This requires context. When our mind doesn't know the context, it subconsciously suggests it to help us out.

For example, take this sentence: "Our department is under budget for the year." You likely had an immediate reaction to that, deciding it was either a positive or negative statement. Sixty-seven percent of the leaders I've given this example to think this statement is positive, because they believe it reflects a cost savings. That is the context their minds created based on their experiences. But I spent much of my career raising money for nonprofits. To me, hearing I'm under budget nearly causes shortness of breath, because it means I didn't raise enough money to keep critical services going. The statement alone is simply a fact; whether we interpreted it as positive or negative is a result of context. If we are not given enough context we create it—and the context we create determines what the experience should mean to us.

The time between gathering information (facts) and determining what they mean to us (context) often gets us in trouble. This is because we add to the story: our fears, our past experiences, or unrelated information. We create noise around what actually happened by creating what it means to us. The closer we stay to facts, the closer we stay to the truth.

Self-awareness encompasses seeing both what is bad and good about ourselves and others. While we can miss the mark with others, we are really bad at evaluating ourselves. Those with the most confidence are among the least self-aware, and those who seem self-aware rank the highest in a negatively skewed self-view. We either forfeit our confidence in the name of humility or our humility in the name of confidence, not understanding that true confidence envelopes humility. The result is that we either miss key mistakes we make, or we spend an excessive amount of time putting ourselves down.

Let's face it: we can be really hard on ourselves. We talk to—and about—ourselves in ways we would never, ever think to speak of others. "Well, that's because I wouldn't want to hurt anyone's feelings," you're thinking. Well, why would you want to hurt your own? When others are hard on themselves, we may agree there are areas to work on, but we remind them of their strengths as well. Do this for yourself! You are not only the sum of your mistakes any more than you are only the sum of your successes.

To be fully self-aware is to understand how we create our thoughts, both negative and positive. It is to challenge our perspective openly and fearlessly, seeking facts and truth despite how it may change our understanding of the world. Challenging our perspective takes patience and courage, but it sets us on the right path to behaviors that create the best possibilities for success.

EXERCISE: WHAT I MADE IT MEAN

Think of a recent conversation or situation that bothered you. Maybe it was a misunderstanding, an argument, or someone behaving in a way that you didn't like. Create three columns and title them, "What Happened," "What I Made it Mean," and "What Else Could it Be?"

In the column titled "What Happened" list only the facts of the situation. What was said? Who said it? What occurred?

Then list what you felt, thought, or interpreted in the "What I Made it Mean" column. Did you think you were right or wrong? What bothered you about the conversation you had? What assumptions did you jump to? And how did it make you feel?

Finally, in the "What Else Could it Be?" column, write what else could have been happening or intended: what did you miss? What was the other person's perspective? What were they experiencing at the time?

Example:

WHAT HAPPENED	WHAT I MADE IT MEAN	WHAT ELSE COULD IT BE?
I received the following email from my boss: "PLEASE DO NOT USE THE OLD COMPANY LOGO IN YOUR CORRESPONDENCE. IT IS CONFUSING TO OUR CUSTOMERS." I went to her office and stated that I didn't know there was a new logo and that I will use it from now on. She thanked me.	1. She's yelling at me (her email was in all caps). 2. She thinks I purposely use the old logo, maybe because she thinks I'm lazy or don't care. 3. She is obsessed with image...our customers don't even notice! 4. She thinks I'm an idiot for not knowing there is a new logo.	1. Maybe she didn't realize her caps lock was on—she's been really hurried lately. 2. It's possible she knows I didn't know about the logo change, and that's why she sent the email. 3. Maybe someone came down on her about the logo and she reacted by sending the email to me (it wasn't personal).

This exercise is a great way to determine how we might be misunderstanding, misinterpreting, or misperceiving the events of our daily life. It provides important insight into the stories we create based solely on our mood, emotions, experiences, or knowledge—stories that are often created without understanding or acknowledgement of what is going on for the other person.

Asking first what the other person might be thinking, feeling, experiencing, or intending can save you from a painful argument.

What We Do: Observable Behavior

Observable behavior is the cornerstone of self-awareness. How we interact with the world around us—how we show up in all areas of our lives—is the living proof of who we are. We are, simply put, the culmination of our actions. Our thoughts inform and lead our behavior, so it is critical to understand how we have developed our thoughts. But our behavior is where we demonstrate who we really are…and who we are becoming. How well do you know either of those persons?

We observe others' behaviors constantly and immediately decide whether we approve or disapprove, what those behaviors mean, and what we should believe about that person. How often do you observe yourself for the same information? How often do you ask yourself how others may interpret your tone, language, or actions? What are you communicating with your behavior? More importantly, is it what you want to communicate?

I have worked with countless leaders who struggle to identify why they experience high turnover, low productivity, or negative feedback from their teams. They have not worked inwardly to assess how their behaviors affect others or what information they are giving others through their actions. You may intend to be supportive of your friends, for example, but if someone can't name a supportive action you've taken (or they have misunderstood how you show support), you have failed to demonstrate this quality.

The first step in observing our behaviors is to define both our current and desired behaviors. Again, this requires you to be vulnerable, honest, and courageous. When we take an inventory of our actions, we often find things we don't like (but we often discover some of our inherent greatness, too!).

EXERCISE: YOUR OBSERVABLE BEHAVIORS

Take time to answer the following questions. These are meant to help you define your current and desired behaviors:

1. What behaviors make up your daily activities?
2. Do you make time for things that are important to you (such as personal or spiritual development, exercise, family, etc.)?
3. How often do you find yourself frustrated by a lack of productivity or achievement at the end of the day?
4. What is your most successful current behavior? How does it enhance your life?
5. How might others misunderstand you? What can you do to address this?
6. What are your top five values? How do your current behaviors demonstrate these values?
7. If someone else wrote your biography, what would you want them to say?
8. Name a behavior you engage in that reflects one of your fears rather than your desired behaviors.
9. Finish this sentence as many times as necessary: I am a person who _____.

Observing our own behavior, while challenging, opens us to understanding how we are demonstrating who we are and what matters to us. It provides ongoing feedback for what we may want to change in the future. If you do not like what you see, what behaviors will help you change it?

When I speak with victims of crime, we often discuss what success may look like following a traumatic event. During most of our lives, certain actions of daily survival are a given. But when our lives are disrupted, we need to redefine what moves us towards healing and resilience. Sometimes it means just getting out of bed. Other times it means getting through a workday without feeling anxious. Crisis and trauma cause chaos in our minds, so success must be defined in tangible, observable terms to ground us. Defining the next right step—the action we need to take in the next five minutes, five hours, or five days—is often what lays the foundation for overcoming significant challenges. We are not resilient just because we think we are. We are not resilient only when we've done something tremendous. We are resilient when we take small, meaningful steps every day that add up over time to a thriving, joyful existence.

Everyday Awareness

When the pandemic began many of us discovered characteristics about ourselves, our teams, and our communities that we didn't previously know. We learned what it meant to isolate ourselves from family, work associates, friends, and our communities. To spend significant amounts of time with just a handful of people whom, though we know and love, we are not accustomed to spending so much time with. We learned what it meant to relate to others in new and digital ways, what it meant to rely on community members we never noticed and now recognized as essential, and how our lives have been built on a world connected by transportation, technology, and efficiency. Some blossomed in this environment, some struggled. Many reached a level of depression they had not previously known, sadly demonstrated by growing numbers of suicidal ideology and completion. We developed, in a short time, a knowledge of our immediate threshold for significant levels of change in a short period of time.

Some of my clients solicited my advice in helping their teams adapt quickly to remote working or other significant changes to their daily operations. I worked with companies to build new systems of accountability and communication to optimize the new work environment. I encouraged flexibility of scheduling and responsibilities where possible to allow those homeschooling children to adjust to their new familial demands. But most importantly, I challenged leaders to be self-aware of their own expectations, fears, and limitations as they determined the best systems for a new working environment.

Unsurprisingly, the teams led by self-aware leaders fared the best in adapting quickly to a new paradigm of leadership. We challenged these leaders' expectations of productivity to streamline the best short-term outcomes given a new and, in many cases, less-than-ideal work environment. Leaders who understood their own style, limitations, and strengths were able to better adapt their leadership strategies for their team's new challenges. They were better prepared to weather the difficulties of working through the pandemic and experienced less traumatic symptoms following the pandemic than those who exhibited lower levels of self-awareness. Most importantly, those who showed high levels of self-awareness experienced the lowest turnover of staff.

If you are aware of your strengths and weaknesses and the role they play in your success, you are far more likely to build teams and systems that support (rather than mirror) your own qualities. When I coach leaders, I ask them to consider the strengths of those around them, name how those strengths differ from their own, and how those differences may be an asset rather than a burden. To understand how others' strengths and perspectives complement our own is to understand how self-awareness enables us to be our personal best in a team environment.

We are great at seeking those who are like us. While it may be human nature, it is not a strength, because it's driven by ego rather than growth. It's easier to stick with those who act like us, think like us, and see the world the same way. It's self-aware to seek out those who act or think differently, and whose strengths are so far from our own that it makes us uncomfortable at times. Self-awareness requires us to vulnerably examine who we are so we can build meaningful relationships with those who are unlike us. It requires us to acknowledge that others possess gifts that we were not bestowed, and likewise acknowledge that we possess unique gifts that others may not recognize or appreciate. It means we engage daily in self-examination and, more importantly, are able to identify the changes we want to make to become the person we want to be.

When we are self-aware, we are not as susceptible to disruption. It is easier for us to accept how others think or behave and adapt our behavior accordingly. It is also how we steadfastly uphold our own values while respecting others: if we are self-aware, we do not require others to understand or agree with us to maintain our beliefs.

This level of self-awareness (and its benefits) is only possible when we persevere at observing our own thoughts and behaviors. Resilient people know who they are. They are willing to be self-reflective, vulnerable, and flexible. They recognize their perspective is unique from others. And most importantly, they know how to remain the person they want to be through life's toughest challenges.

For reflection

Answer the following questions alone or with your team:

1. How important do you think self-awareness is to your success?
2. What changes would you like to make based on how others might observe you?
3. How might you be unaware of others' perspectives in your daily interactions?
4. What would you like to learn about yourself?
5. Name five of your personal strengths. Identify how they help you and others be more successful.

PRINCIPLE THREE:

MINDSET IS A CHOICE

Between stimulus and response, there is a space. In that space is our power to choose our response. In our response lies our growth and our freedom.

—Victor E. Frankl

Two Erasers

Nancy Regan made me cry.

Not *that* Nancy Regan, though we were enamored with our version since, just weeks before, our new president was inaugurated. Having the same name as the new First Lady made our own Nancy Regan a very popular girl in my kindergarten class.

She asked to use my eraser and, though hesitant, I handed it to her (I wasn't about to make the popular girl mad). It was brand new, and I always loved those large, pink rectangles when they were fresh, before they had any marks or dents on it. She furiously scrubbed her paper, removing her imperfection and, in the process, broke the eraser in two.

I can't exactly say why this was so devastating to me (I was six), but I felt hot tears pooling behind my eyes. I took the broken pieces in my little hands and sat quietly while the fat, silent tears rolled down my cheeks. The teacher's new assistant, a college student we saw twice a week and loved for her youthful personality, came quickly to my desk.

"What's wrong, Julie?" she asked with genuine concern.

"My eraser. It's brand new, and it's broken," I lamented.

Without a beat she simply said, "that's ok. Now you have two!"

My little mind was blown. *Wow! Why didn't I think of that?* I thought. I smiled up at her gratefully for this little insight. I happily went back to my work, feeling lucky that I now had double the number of erasers I had just minutes earlier.

It's been more than four decades since that silly conversation, but I remember it as a life-changing moment (we have no idea the profound impact our words can have on others, particularly children). She was the first person to teach me that attitude is a *choice*. That my problem is only half the challenge: the other half is how I choose to look at it. Often, when I'm stuck on a problem, I laughingly think of that moment and ask myself, "how might I now have two erasers?"

Hundreds of studies have been conducted to determine the impact mindset, attitude, or positive thinking have on our overall wellbeing. We know that a positive mindset keeps us healthier: it improves our brain function, lowers risk of cardiovascular events, and even improves our immune system. Positive thinking also has profound mental health benefits. In one study, researchers found that when clients replaced negative thoughts with positive ones—even positive thoughts unrelated to the original worries that triggered the negative thoughts—they experienced a significant reduction in anxiety and excessive worry.[2] If resilience speaks to our ability to navigate and overcome life's challenges, removing the power anxiety and worry hold over our minds is one of our greatest resilience builders.

Human history is replete with stories of individuals overcoming significant obstacles through their mindset. These are our heroes: those who overcome poverty, disaster, impediments, illiteracy, disease, and much more through perseverance and self-belief. We admire them, commend them, and retell their stories, but we don't often adapt their practices to our own lives. We

---

2   C. Eagleson, S. Hayes, A. Mathews, G. Perman, C. Hirsch. *"The power of positive thinking: Pathological worry is reduced by thought replacement in Generalized Anxiety Disorder."* In *Behaviour Research and Therapy 78 (2016) 13-18. Elsevier.*

believe, for some strange reason, that their magic is beyond our grasp. Resilient people know that most of our heroes don't possess anything special. They just tried a little harder, believed a little more, or stayed a little longer than the rest of us. That's the power of a great mindset.

For many years, scientists believed that certain groups of people were more physiologically prone to be good at running than others. They believed these people possessed something others didn't: a secret gene, a lack of pain, or some other phenomenon that might give them the edge of distance or speed. Now we know these groups, such as the Tarahumara people of northwestern Mexico, simply *choose* to be good at running. Running is woven into their cultural, spiritual, and familial practices. Unlike American marathons, which tend to be individually focused, they consider running a bonding community event. They are not physiologically different than anyone else; they just prioritize running as part of their lifestyle. They are raised to believe that running is fun and meaningful, and this mindset produces some of the world's greatest distance runners. While individuals have unique traits and gifts, it is far more often that, like the Tarahumara, our attitude about a particular subject drives us to succeed.

How Others Frame Our Mindset

What others believe about us—and project onto us—can play a powerful role in our mindset. While we are ultimately responsible for our self-view and the mindset we choose, it's also important to acknowledge that we are part of a greater human family, and that family affects how we see ourselves. This is especially true for children, who look to others in early years to tell them who they are and what mindset they should possess.

When I was young, I rarely thought about my intelligence. I received good grades and school was easy for me, but as a "social butterfly" I was known more for my emotional intelligence than my book smarts. This persona was encouraged by my family, friends, and school, so I didn't second-guess it.

In fifth grade, however, I was placed into a program for gifted students, and for the first time I considered I might have academic gifts. I enjoyed the program, held with a small group of students who met weekly at the convent alongside my Catholic school. The nun in charge of the program was jovial and fun; though the class was rigorous, she made the sessions seem like a field trip full of new and interesting ideas. I loved the in-depth dive into a variety of subjects, and I thrived in the small-group environment.

In my regular classes we were learning long division. I had a strange and pervasive mental block against this form of math (one I overcame eventually), and it led to a deeper distaste for math in general. Through no fault of his, many of the nights my father spent working with me on my math skills ended in my frustration and tears, increasing my belief that I would never understand it. Meanwhile the teacher who had recommended me for the gifted program doubted my difficulties with the subject. She accused me of not trying, of not caring, and of not wanting to work hard. Her criticism became worse and more public, finally resulting in her berating me in front of my classmates. The more she pushed, the worse my mental block against math became. At home, I cried more and more until I eventually shut down. My parents tried to intervene, explaining to the teacher that I was truly struggling and could benefit from some help. She didn't seem to believe them. Eventually, to punish me for my "lack of effort," she pulled me from the gifted program. That was the last time I believed I was smart.

Luckily, other than mild embarrassment, I don't remember this having a significant impact on my self-esteem. I just figured I was better at the arts, writing, a few sports, and socializing. Those were my gifts. I still received good grades, so I didn't worry about it. I went on this way through high school and college, believing I was "smart enough" but never taking more difficult or accelerated classes because, as I learned in fifth grade, those weren't for me. I didn't have the mindset of someone intelligent. I had the mindset of someone creative and artistic, someone kind and empathetic, someone hardworking. But not smart.

I was in my forties before the question of my intelligence came up again. I was required to take an intensive, three-hour intelligence test for a job position. As I entered the testing room, I laughed to myself, thinking if I had to take an IQ test, it was good I had already been offered the job!

I completed the test early and suspected I had done something wrong. I had never taken an IQ test of any kind; surely, I missed something. I reviewed my answers, but didn't have any changes, so I turned in the test. The facilitator raised his eyebrows, said nothing, and said he'd be back after he scanned the test into the computerized scoring system. A while later he returned, smiling.

"Have you ever taken an IQ test?" he asked.

"No, why?" I felt embarrassment rising in my cheeks. He was clearly about to deliver bad news. Maybe I had taken it wrong. Maybe I didn't even understand the questions. I bit my lip.

"You scored one of the highest scores I've ever seen," he said. "You're in the top 3% of adults tested."

I blinked. "Are you sure? Maybe the system scored it incorrectly…"

"No," he said. "I ran it twice and then looked over it myself. This is your score."

I stared at the paper in disbelief. Never once did occurred to me I had any level of intelligence beyond average. I thanked him, left, and sat in my car for a bit. I felt sad and strange. It took me a moment to recognize what I was feeling: it was grief.

Like any child, I considered a variety of careers throughout my youth. When I was eight, I wanted to be a saint, until someone explained to me that that wasn't a profession (though I wouldn't give up on that idea until I learned that to be a saint, I'd also have to be dead, so that no longer sounded like a promising choice). In sixth grade I wanted to be a newspaper editor, in eight grade a psychologist. In high school a doctor, professor, actress, or fighter pilot (somehow these all carried equal weight for consideration). I talked myself out of three of these because they required intelligence. Smart people were doctors and professors. People good at math and physics could be fighter pilots. I didn't have those skills.

I made so many choices—not just concerning my career—based on what I believed my limitations were. What if I had believed I was smart? What could I have accomplished? While I was happy and grateful for the career I had, it was difficult to wonder what could've been. And more broadly, to wonder how many other people experience their version of the IQ test sometime in their lives: that moment when we realize we are more than anyone led us to believe.

You Can't—or Won't?

Anthony,[3] a client with new leadership responsibilities whom I was asked to assist as he adjusted to a new and difficult role, placed his face in his hands and groaned.

"I don't have the personality or credibility," he sighed. "I just don't know if I can do this."

"Then you won't," I said, pragmatically.

He stared at me in disbelief, perhaps waiting to see if I would change my statement. After all, it was my job to motivate him, right?

As a software engineer, Anthony spent much of his career working alone, only reporting to others when it was necessary for project completion. He had no experience leading a team or employees that, in some cases, were more experienced and knowledgeable than he. But he had been recently thrust into a leadership position when his department's leader unexpectedly passed away. The firm's partners recognized Anthony's potential and talent and tapped him to step into his former colleague's role. Though he had always wanted to lead a team, Anthony feared assuming the role of a colleague who was well-liked and deeply missed. He did not want to try to fill those shoes.

"You don't understand. I can't lead like Jim did..."

---

3   *Name and minor details have been changed to protect client privacy.*

"Then don't," I interrupted. "Lead like *you* do."

He thought about this for a moment. When he became the department's leader, he assumed he was asked to step into the role because he shared certain traits with the former leader, Jim. They were both focused and reliable. They had the same degrees and similar work experience. But that's where the similarities ended: Jim was a charismatic extrovert who inspired his team, while Anthony was an introvert who favored quietly leading by example. Anthony thought the department would want someone just like Jim, knowing how much they all missed him.

We talked about his leadership style and how it differed from Jim's. That it was okay that it was different because each leader has unique strengths. He was in a difficult position: Jim didn't leave, he was gone. Everyone felt it and grieved the loss, and it would take time for them to adjust to both their loss and to a new leader. That would require patience and empathy on Anthony's part, but it certainly didn't mean he couldn't succeed in his new role.

"What if leading like Jim would only make this harder?" I suggested. "What if your strength is that you *aren't* like Jim, so your department still gets a great leader while holding their memory of Jim in its own, unique place?"

Anthony smiled. He hadn't thought of it that way and was appreciative of this new perspective.

"You sure know how to spin things," he laughed.

"Not spin…reframe," I said, chuckling.

I explained that we have a choice in how we view and respond to every scenario; that we make choices in every moment (whether we are conscious of them or not). When life deals us lemons, we must *choose* to make lemonade. For those who have natural resilience, this choice is easier. They quickly identify the opportunity in every situation, focusing on what *isn't* permanent rather than what is. For those who struggle with resilience, this is harder because they must fight feelings of apathy or helplessness.

Anthony and I discussed a plan for reframing his mindset. We discussed how he could leverage his unique strengths with his team, building on Jim's legacy with space to establish new goals and culture. How this challenge was an opportunity to learn about himself, his goals, and his leadership style. Anthony reframed his thinking and looked at his new position as an opportunity to develop himself and his team. He had great ideas for the department, and we worked to keep those front-of-mind. He focused on setting goals and celebrating achievements. He didn't waste any more time worrying about what he *wasn't* (a leader like Jim) but what he *was*: a consistent, supportive leader who set a great example of integrity for his team. Four years later, he still manages the group, has grown his team from five to twenty, and is on partner track at his firm.

The Half Glass

For a good part of my life, I thought positive thinking was a myth. I believed positivity was an easy way out; that those who "looked on the bright side" were, frankly, somewhat deluding themselves. Meeting people I would now define as toxically positive didn't help. "Toxic positivity" is a phenomenon in which people focus exclusively on the positive and minimize or dismiss the negative (you'll learn more about toxic positivity later). However well-intended, the dismissal of others' pain and difficulties is harmful. I struggled for a long time to find the merits of positive thinking because I feared overlooking reality, being toxically positive, or taking the easy way out. My view of positivity was, well, pretty negative.

Working with victims of violence reminded me constantly just how dark and hopeless life can feel. Anyone who works in crisis response, law enforcement, healthcare, social work, or a related service field sees life's cruelty on a frequent basis. Life is hard. It bites. It stings. But if we hang in there, it also sings. I saw many, many people overcome violence and tragedy to hear that music. I watched them struggle out of unimaginable circumstances, one step at a time, to reestablish their lives. In my research I've asked more than five hundred individuals how they overcame significant hardships like violence, grief, bankruptcy, and disease. Nearly a third said, "I didn't have a choice." But they did. Whether they realized it or not, they *chose* survival. They got back up when others would've stayed down. Survival is a miracle that I was lucky enough to witness every day. I learned from these individuals that they emerged from their darkness through hope, perseverance, and, most importantly, by focusing relentlessly on a good outcome. That's when I began to understand the power of a positive mindset.

I am pragmatic by nature, so I understand why it's difficult for some to see the glass as "half-full" rather than "half-empty." That's ok: there's merit in seeing it half-empty, too. Those who see the glass as half-empty are realistic and, in many cases, aware of opportunities that more optimistic thinking might miss. Both ways of thinking are acceptable and beneficial. That's what I mean by choosing our mindset: we determine for ourselves how we will use the information and opportunities all around us. I choose to find merit in both ways of looking at life. The glass can be half-empty or half-full. It doesn't really matter. The more important question is, *what are you going to do with it?*

Even if you consider yourself an optimist, you choose negativity far more often than you might realize. That's by design: your brain is programmed to think that way. You begin life seeing the glass as half-empty, because your brain's survival mechanism needs to assess regularly what it will need to stay nourished and safe. Your brain assesses everything in your environment for potential dangers. It looks for what is missing so it knows what it must secure for survival. Seeing the glass half-full is a learned response, introduced to you at some point in your life. That's the beauty of our minds: they are brilliantly mailable. We can rewire new pathways at any time, developing new thoughts and perspectives. We can acknowledge that we're not likely to go thirsty anytime soon and see fullness in the glass. And we can use our mind's natural pessimism to our advantage, recognizing the potential dangers ahead to seek the inherent opportunities within.

Think about your annual employment review. No matter how highly you score, what praise you receive, or what metrics you exceed, what do you usually notice first? Right: you zero in on the worst part. Depending on your nature, you might even think about it for hours afterwards, wondering either how you will fix it or how the person evaluating you got it so wrong. What if you looked at all the positives and thought, "Wow, I'm doing pretty well, all things considered. I just need to make a few adjustments."

It doesn't negate the fact that you have work to do. It simply allows you to include your strengths in your mental download of this information, providing you a perspective that is closer to the truth.

Some people harm their performance by over-focusing on the negative feedback in their reviews. They spend so much time and energy focusing on fixing what is wrong that they steal time and efficiency from what is going well. A year later they may have improved what they needed to work on, but they now have new areas of growth to worry about. By acknowledging the positive, you develop plans that not only addresses any problems but give equal attention to keeping the good. In other words, a positive mindset helps you not only look at things optimistically, but more realistically as well.

Voltaire once said, "perfect is the enemy of good." I keep this saying on a sticky note above my computer because—I admit—I am a recovering perfectionist. Perfectionism is simply a euphemism for failing to launch. Perfectionists will sit on go, engines revved, waiting for the right moment with the right preparation to do the right thing. Guess what? That moment never comes. Meanwhile, the world passes us by, heeding all the riches and successes that "good" deserves. Life is messy, chaotic, and imperfect. Success only comes when we live it well anyway.

Resilience loves "good" and "good enough." It understands that there are no rules about how to live your best life—there's what works for us, and what doesn't. The better you can identify more than one answer to life's most pressing questions, the more resilient you become. It is easier to be told how to act, what to think, and how to live. But by digging into our hardest challenges, developing multiple ways of looking at each for its opportunities, we find our way to both the best answers for us and the perseverance to carry it out.

Who says?

There is a single question I ask anyone who is struggling against perfection or a perfectionist mindset: *Who says?* You think being a good employee means working tons of overtime? *Who says?* That you have to climb the corporate ladder because you got that degree? *Who says?* That success is defined by driving a specific car or living in a particular zip code? *Who says?* That being a good parent or partner means your house is always clean? *Who says?* (I'd argue for a little bit messy and having more fun!).

Most of the time, we conform so quickly to society's expectations—or what we *think* those expectations are—that we forget to ask who we're doing it for. Why are you keeping up with the Jones's? *Who says* they're doing it right, anyway? Ask yourself often who's standards you are seeking to live up to and why they matter. No one else makes the rules on what makes us happy. You do. You don't owe an explanation to anyone for how you become your personal best. Life does not guarantee your happiness. It guarantees it will provide the lessons that teach you how to be happy. Moments of emptiness and despair help create a better life, to grow into who you are meant to be. Choosing the right mindset means choosing to use all the information life is giving you—positive and negative—to create the best outcome.

The Purpose of Failure

Failure is one of life's greatest gifts. It forges the strongest mind, the greatest will, the most successful processes. Yet we fear failure so intensely that some scientists believe we all experience atychiphobia—the intense fear of failure—at least once in our lives. This phobia occurs when our fear of failure becomes so great that a consistent, paralyzing feeling of dread keeps us from taking action. It is powerful, overwhelming, and haunting. It brings down great people just before their greatest moments. But it doesn't have to. We can choose to see failure quite differently. Instead of giving up, I ask my clients to "rethink" failure. What purpose is failure serving you? *What are you meant to learn from it?*

In consulting with educators, I have discovered that our youth are becoming increasingly less resilient. This is attributable to many factors—socioeconomic concerns, living in a fast-paced digital world, increases in clinical anxiety and depression, extreme schedules, and more—but one particularly alarming reason for this drop in resilience is because we no longer *allow* our children to fail. I spoke to nearly fifty educators who report a near-paralyzing fear of failure among 9th and 10th grade students. When I dug in to learn more, I discovered that in many cases, the students simply lacked meaningful experience with failure.

In recent decades, our society has significantly shifted activities and experiences to shield children from pain and boost their self-worth. We have chosen confidence over resilience, forgetting that confidence is built *through* resilience. "Helicopter parenting" earned its name from parents who, with good intent, want to protect their children from harm, failure, and disappointment. But disappointment and failure are a necessary part of life. They teach valuable and lasting lessons. Preventing children from experiencing failure sets them up for incorrect expectations and prevents them from developing the resilience to succeed later in life.

I helped an instructor in one district develop a gentle but effective exercise in which her ninth-grade students experienced failure. We set them up to fail intentionally with an unexpectedly difficult task. Their nervousness was evident early-on, but we let them experience failure and then discussed the experience. We talked about the anxiety they felt when they suspected failure was imminent, how they felt while trying to complete the task, and how it felt to fail. Most importantly, we *normalized* failure as an expected outcome of the task.

We then discussed how to see the failure as an opportunity to try something different. They tried it again, and a third time. By the end of the third time, the students not only no longer feared the chance of failure (in fact, they neutrally anticipated it) but had developed systems in their small groups to overcome problems if failure occurred again. They learned quickly that failure was only elimination of what didn't work to achieve the task at hand.

We must commit to the mindset that **failure is useful.** Failure is a gift: it's what doesn't work getting out of our way so we can discover what will. Thinking differently about failure isn't easy. It requires discipline, a positive mindset, and creativity. As Albert Einstein said, "you never fail until you stop trying." He also said, "anyone who has never made a mistake has never tried anything new," and "failure is success in progress." It seems he thought a lot about—and likely experienced—failure often. Why? Because he tried often. And, as one of the most brilliant and accomplished minds in history, he succeeded often.

If we retool our mindset about failure, we see it for its learning opportunities, problem-solving information, and as a chance to perfect the imperfect. We don't get it right the first time. We're not meant to. To master something, we must spend thousands of hours doing it (science is still arguing just how many hours, but let's say it's safely in the thousands). What's interesting is that the number of mental hours—the practice of visualizing the task and envisioning success—is also extremely powerful. One study showed that "mental contractions" of two muscle groups resulted in increased strength, where those who performed no physical or mental contractions experienced no change.[4] In other words, the participants just thinking about moving their finger or elbow caused an increase in strength! This required training: in this case for 15 minutes a day over 12 weeks—which means it is necessary to repeatedly ask our minds to perform a task before we succeed. How often do we fail simply because we gave up before our minds mastered the task?

The Resilient Mindset

When it comes to choosing your mindset, you act alone. *You* choose what you believe about yourself, your life, your opportunities, and

4   Eagleson, S. Hayes, A. Mathews, G. Perman, C. Hirsch. *"The power of positive thinking: Pathological worry is reduced by thought replacement in Generalized Anxiety Disorder."* In *Behaviour Research and Therapy 78 (2016) 13-18.* Elsevier.

Ranganathan VK, Siemionow V, Liu JZ, Sahgal V, Yue GH. *"From mental power to muscle power-gaining strength by using the mind."* Neuropsychologia. 2004;42(7):944-56. doi: 10.1016/j.neuropsychologia.2003.11.018.

your failures. *You* decide what will hold you back or when you will persevere. And you—*and only you*—are accountable for your actions. Though you may be a victim of circumstances, you choose how you view those circumstances and what you're going to do about it. I am eternally grateful that there are people to help, and that humans are built to lean upon one another. We all should both offer and receive help. But ultimately, how you view the world and act within it is yours to choose.

Resilience is built upon the choices you make regarding the circumstances you are faced with. Your ability to persevere is directly in proportion to your beliefs about the challenge at hand, and your ability to overcome challenges directly in proportion to your mindset. But in recent decades, society has increasingly told us that others should manage our emotions or wellbeing. Nothing could be further from the truth: not only is it dangerous to hand over our wellness to others, it's impossible. When we hold others responsible to do the hard work for us, to protect our feelings from being hurt, or provide opportunities for us to thrive, we hand over our personal control to them. And for those who feel responsible to do this for others, we are setting ourselves up for a codependent loop that will be impossible to complete because we do not hold that much power over anyone but ourselves. In other words, **no one can make you miserable without your permission, or successful without your participation.**

A resilient mindset requires dedication to the thoughts we have and the behavior those thoughts develop. It requires us to be radically accountable for all that we think, do, say, and believe. When we hold ourselves accountable for our own thoughts and behaviors, we begin to see how powerful we really are in creating and changing our lives. We don't wait for others to act for us; we intuitively know that we are responsible for our happiness, wellness, and fulfillment.

This mindset is only possible when we find the opportunity in every challenge instead of the shame of failure or the anxiety of defeat. When we are beholden to the most positive outcome. And when we choose to believe in ourselves, showing up every day as our best selves, confident and rooted in our purpose.

For Reflection

1. Think about what the life you desire requires of you. What beliefs will get you there? What changes do you need to make to your attitude or mindset to help you reach your goals?
2. Make a list of your most pervasive negative thoughts. What positive thoughts can replace each of them?
3. What does a resilient mindset mean to you? What characteristics of resilience would you like to possess?
4. Name one way you use failure to your advantage. If you can't think of any, what steps will you take to start?

Extra Credit

In her exceptional book, *Mindset: Changing the way you think to fulfil your potential,* Dr. Carol S. Dweck introduces us to "fixed" and "growth" mindsets. Dweck outlines a powerful case for the growth mindset, reminding us how our choice of either mindset creates our reality. I recommend reading this book and spending time with her insights and questions, determining how you will develop your growth mindset.

PRINCIPLE FOUR:

GRATITUDE IS THE ANTIDOTE TO SUFFERING

Gratitude is the sign of noble souls.

—Aesop

Unexpected Gratitude

On a warm, late afternoon in May of 2011, the residents of Joplin, Missouri were going about their weekend business. As high school graduation concluded, hundreds of happy students and families splayed out onto the high school grounds, chatting about dinner, graduation parties, and the future. Streets hummed with traffic going to and from dinner, stores, and last-minute tasks before the work week ahead. These are the normal sounds of a midwestern spring weekend.

Around 5:40 pm, these familiar, happy sounds were shattered by the wailing of tornado sirens. Residents headed for their basements, closets, or bathrooms. Stores corralled shoppers into designated storm areas. Cars pulled off the side of the road or under overpasses. Everyone crouched, protected, and waited. For Missourians, this is an inconvenient but not uncommon practice, one we don't usually respond to with too much concern.

Within just minutes of the siren, an EF-5 tornado—one of the worst to ever hit an American town—ripped through the heart of Joplin. Residents didn't have time to prepare, though it wouldn't have mattered: the sheer power and force of the tornado was more than most structures could withstand. The tornado seized the town for thirty-eight terrifying, unforgiving minutes. When it finally subsided, it had taken 161 lives, injured 1,150 more, and leveled thousands of houses and community strongholds. The hospital was devastated along with two fire stations, immobilizing a majority of first responders. The high school, still buzzing from graduation, was destroyed. Helpless, the community clung to hope, prayer, and each other as they emerged from underground to find their town completely transformed.

280 miles away in St. Louis, I watched coverage of the tornado from the safety of my clear-skied home. As a trained crisis responder and social service leader, I knew I would be receiving a call shortly to assist in the response. When that call came, I didn't know it would put gratitude front-and-center in my research on resilience.

Soon after that call, my colleague and I arrived in Joplin. We surveyed the town before reporting to the makeshift command center (a youth recreation center-turned-response center for the community), hoping to gain an understanding of what those we were going to meet had seen, heard, and witnessed. The physics of a tornado are strange: a single sink standing with nothing else discernable that a house once stood around it. A baby car seat impaled by a tree branch still attached to the tree. Cars turned upside down or thrust into walls at an angle. Trees (the few of them left, anyway) raw from having been stripped of all bark and leaves.

People sat on porches of what used to be their homes or picked through rubble to find remnants of their lives. Street names were spraypainted onto the streets because there were no longer street signs and, worse, no recognizable landmarks. First responders— called in from surrounding towns, cities, and states—worked to restore services, recover remains, and assist residents while a variety of crews established makeshift work zones. With billions in damages, this was the U.S.'s costliest tornado in history and there was a lot to be done to restore the community's infrastructure back into working conditions.

Our job, on the other hand, was restoring the human condition. We are psychological first responders, helping community members navigate the first steps of restoring their lives following crisis. We accompanied several community members through the process of getting a variety of needs met: food, temporary shelter, applications for longer-term housing, lost medication, transportation, replacement identification documents, etc. while simultaneously identifying mental health and wellness needs.

The stories we heard were remarkable, tragic, and life changing. We met many people who lost everything. Others lost more: parents, siblings, friends, and even children. Hundreds of community members were processed through the center, all of them seeking resources, guidance, and respite. Some just wanted food, water, and rest. Others, someone to bear witness to their suffering; to make it real and meaningful.

I anticipated that the residents of Joplin and surrounding areas would be understandably tired, confused, frustrated, and grieving. That they would be experiencing despair and hopelessness, sprinkled with anger and anxiety. And they were all these things. What I did not anticipate is that they were also remarkably, memorably grateful.

As I navigated the center each day, I heard hundreds of discussions about what people were grateful for. That they had a relative nearby they could stay with until they found a new home. That a charitable organization was able to provide food, clothing, or a hotel room. That they lost this, but not that. That they had insurance or other housing on its way. That they still had a place to work. That they had access to food, clothing, and medical attention. That they had their lives. That they lost someone, but that person did not suffer. And on and on. These exceptional people, in an unimaginable situation, said thank you to everyone, speaking specifically and at length about their gratitude. They were patient and kind to one another as they waited in one line after another for a variety of resources. They understood what it means to be part of a community, and that gratitude is a feeling best experienced in the company of others.

One afternoon I was asked to join a social service agency for a small ceremony to give cash-equivalency cards to those who needed them. When the volunteers presented these to the residents, they thanked each of them. I don't mean the recipients thanked them (though they did)—I mean those *gifting* the money thanked each recipient for "allowing them the honor of serving their community members." Not a single recipient was dry-eyed.

This single, humble act, particularly after witnessing days of unbridled gratitude, was game-changing for me. I had responded to other crises, but none had been this devastating to the community. And yet, I had never felt such hope for them. I had never seen people so joyful about serving others, nor recipients of help so sure they were going to make it with the help of others. Their resilience was evident because their gratitude was clear. While it was a long, difficult road, with the grief of the lives lost now woven into history, the town of Joplin was rebuilt. The high school, hospital, library, and other community anchors updated to new, beautiful facilities. Homes were rebuilt or relocated. Memorials were erected and vigils are still held to commemorate those lost. Community members remember how they came together to grieve, hope, and, most of all, became resilient together.

Since my time in Joplin, I have interviewed several survivors of crisis about the role gratitude played in their healing. I have asked crisis responders their thoughts on the relationship between resilience and gratitude. I have read studies, documented random acts of gratitude, and worked with leaders to utilize practices of gratitude in their quest for team resilience. Across the board, each of these individuals, as well as the outcomes of grateful acts, confirm an undeniable link between feelings of gratitude and the ability to be resilient. Science backs this up: more and more studies are conducted annually to understand and confirm the relationship between gratitude and wellness.

Our Minds on Gratitude

The effect gratitude has on our thinking is profound and undeniable. Thinking about what we're grateful for helps boost good endorphins, keeps us focused on abundance rather than scarcity, and enhances our brain's ability to recognize positive patterns that lead to continued positive outcomes. In dozens of scientific studies on the subject, those who can articulate what they are grateful for show improved mental health. These benefits are available to all of us, regardless of experiences with significant challenges. But for those who experience trauma, anxiety, and substance abuse, gratitude plays a unique and critical role in our ability to heal. A 2017 study on the effects of resilience and gratitude on victims of a campus shooting[5] showed that, while resilience was an important quality in being able to withstand trauma, *gratitude* had a specific

---

5 Vieselmeyer, J., Holguin, J., & Mezulis, A. (2017). "The role of resilience and gratitude in post-traumatic stress and growth following a campus shooting." *Psychological Trauma: Theory, Research, Practice, and Policy, 9(1), 62–69.*

role in increasing the occurrence of post-traumatic growth (positive changes that result from experiences with trauma and stress).

Neuroplasticity is amazing. It's our brain's way of adapting to new stimuli, environments, behaviors, and information. Our brain can change function and structure to meet the demands of our lives. This happens whether we want it to or not; why not choose to use it to our advantage? Each time we take on a new challenge, our brain pulls from previous resources while looking for new ones. If we have trained our brain to remember and capitalize on positive thoughts, it will seek more positivity. If we have trained it to focus on the negative, negativity is what it will find. The point is, you can choose to rewire your mind in new ways, focusing on recalling the information you want to. Choosing positive thoughts, particularly those linked to gratitude and community, plays an important role in a resilient mindset.

While scientists are still learning more about *why* there is a positive correlation between gratitude and mental health, stress reduction, wellness, life fulfillment, and more, they know there is a correlation. That's enough for me to encourage you to use grateful thoughts to your advantage!

EXERCISE: LOVE GRATITUDE

When you think of what you're grateful for, what do you feel? Among the first words that come to mind for most is "love." Love is arguably the most significant positive force in our lives, and along with its nemesis (fear), guides most of our thoughts and actions. It is easy, then, to use "L-O-V-E" as an acronym for the gratitude process:

Look. Notice what there is to be grateful for all around you: relationships, nature, abundance, faith, food, health, and more. Most of us falter at this stage—it's not that there isn't plenty to be grateful for, but that we simply don't notice in the grind of daily life. Remember: our minds are programmed for the negative, so it's easier to notice what *isn't* working. We have to make an effort to notice what is.

Observe. Determine *why* you are grateful for the person, thing, or place you noticed. This is a step farther than simply looking—it is knowing *what* you're looking for and *why* it matters. It means developing the questions that help you appreciate at a deeper level: what qualities do I appreciate about this person? What growth is possible in this scenario? What do I like about this meal? What do I feel about being in this place? In other words, be specific about what you are noticing. Be granular with your appreciation.

Validate. Make the connection between this person, place, thing, or scenario and your values. What is it about this that connects to who you are or who you want to be? Do you appreciate this person because they help you be a better person, or possess qualities that enhance your life? Do you like this work because you feel purposeful and appreciated? What does your appreciation tell you about who you are, your values, or your desires? Most importantly, how will continuing to fill your life with persons, things, places, or circumstances like this help you be your best self?

Experience. Keep doing what makes you happy! It's really that simple. Once you determine what, who, and where feeds your soul, give it more of the same. Too often we lose sight of what is fun, fulfilling, and important to us in exchange for what is necessary, and it leads to burnout and depression. Engage in the practice of gratitude, which includes continuing what works while looking for new things to be grateful for. Experience new things also: as you know, people who focus on good experiences are more likely to feel happy and have lower anxiety.

The LOVE process helps you build gratitude into your daily life. Over time, the "observe" and "validate" steps become much easier, naturally flowing into what you notice and the experiences you plan for yourself. Remember the magic of spontaneity in this process: often the best moments are those that are unexpected and unplanned. Remember to look everywhere for things to be grateful for.

Gratitude is Not Toxic Positivity

Ever met someone who seems *too* positive? As though they are unable to see the downside or refuse to look at critical details? You may have been dealing with toxic positivity. Toxic positivity is the diminishment, dismissal, or denial of negative emotions to focus on the positive. It rejects reality and, in the context of mental health and relationships, is recognized as a form of gaslighting and abuse. Ignoring the stress, trauma, or pain of others—or ourselves—is toxic and counterproductive. Those who engage in this practice often do so to avoid the discomfort of talking about or dealing with challenges, to "get over it" instead of necessary processing or healing, or at worst, to minimize others' experiences.

Toxic positivity takes on many forms. It may come from good intent but is almost always harmful to the recipient. I have watched leaders minimize or ignore employee's experiences with family death, critically sick children, or personal illness because they wanted them to focus on being productive in the workplace. I have listened to coworkers dismiss someone's significant obstacles or deep anxieties as a simply a "reason to persevere." Once, I even heard someone say the mother of a homicide victim "will be ok because she has other children." People can say truly hurtful, dismissive things in the name of "positivity." Blindly or carelessly focusing on the positive, without empathy and understanding, is devastating and counterproductive.

Gratitude—and resilience—is not about dismissing the negative but focusing on both positive and negative and gleaning helpful details from both. We will inevitably experience significant challenges throughout our lives, but we can be grateful for (1) what we have that is going well, and (2) the significant growth our challenges provide us. In her book *The Gratitude Diaries: How a Year Looking on the Bright Side Can Transform your Life,* author Janice Kaplan explored positive thinking and gratitude for a year and outlined its impact on her thinking. She notes that gratitude does not remove challenges, but changes how they affect us: "The tragic, sad, unexpected, and irritating do take place, and our lives are not necessarily better for them. But our only choice is how to respond. Instead of being masterful at misery, we can become experts at gratitude. After a year of focusing on the bright side, I knew it was a lot more satisfying to be grateful than wrapped up on your own pain."

Wrapped up in our own pain, while our default emotional setting, is a calling for us to overcome. As mentioned previously, our mind gravitates naturally toward the negative. To protect us it seeks what is missing, broken, or dangerous. The choice to override this natural inclination is ours. Beginning with the conscious act of identifying and focusing on the positive attributes of a situation, we signal our brain to capture the good alongside the bad. Eventually we rewire our brains, forming new habits that require less effort to notice the positive.

In the same way we build gratitude through our ability to recall positive attributes of a situation, relationship, or person, so too do we build resilience through our ability to recall positive actions. We remember how we overcame a tough situation the last time, leaning into grateful thoughts of survival and healing. We use this information to overcome the next obstacle, building new tools of resilience, and so on.

EXERCISE: POSITIVE RECALL

Answer the following questions, focusing on specific personal or professional examples:

1. Name a current challenge in your life that, though difficult, you are grateful for.
2. Name a time when you realized after a significant challenge that it was one of the best experiences of your life. Why was it so pivotal or important?
3. What is your mindset about challenges? Do they keep you down, stall you, or excite you?
4. Name three past challenges that you can now, in retrospect, identify the life lessons they were teaching you.
5. What challenge did you give yourself just to see if you could overcome it (i.e., running a marathon, writing a

book, etc.). How did you do? What did you learn about yourself?

The Importance of Mindfulness

I bet you've heard of mindfulness: at work, online, in faith communities, through promoted apps, on social media…my watch even reminds me to be mindful! It's everywhere, and for good reason. It is a great way to center ourselves, manage difficult emotions, and mitigate stress.

Mindfulness isn't new; in fact, it's as old as humanity, but it is experiencing a revival as we learn the importance of disconnecting from and stress and anxiety. Mindfulness includes spiritual practices such as prayer, meditation, chanting, and repetitive spiritual phrases, and the more tactical practices of cognitive focus, breathing, and movement. In whatever way you choose to be mindful, it is an important and helpful step in increasing your gratitude. So while this book doesn't focus on developing mindfulness, I highly recommend you learn more about it and integrate it into your gratitude practice.

Simply put, mindfulness is the ability to be fully aware and engaged in the present moment. When mindful we are focused on the task, conversation, or circumstances of the moment—not our stressors, anxieties, challenges, or anticipated events. Instead, we are aware of what we are doing *now* (and only now), with no regard to five minutes ago or in the future. A popular way of approaching mindfulness is to think of eating a piece of chocolate: most of us absentmindedly eat it, like the taste, and enjoy the sugar kick. We may notice the flavor momentarily, but we're more likely focusing on eating another piece! Instead, imagine you are eating it with full concentration on the chocolate itself: how it smells, its texture, notes of sweetness or bitterness, how crunchy or chewy it is, whether it melts quickly, and how long it takes to eat a small bite. Notice whether you like this piece or not, whether you'd prefer something with it (caramel? Salt?) and what you think about its taste. Now you have a different idea of chocolate, one that is appreciative of its complexity. If you were focusing deeply with me on this just now, you may have noticed that you forgot about everything else in your world for the moment (except, maybe, thoughts of finding some chocolate!). That is what mindfulness feels like. It envelopes us, however temporarily, in now. Many people describe it as being in "the zone." It happens when we do something we love like playing games, sports, music, or art. And it is a necessary process for brain development and critical for gathering data for gratitude.

When we are mindful throughout our day, we notice things we otherwise would miss. The flowers blooming nearby; the happiness of a dog going for a walk with its owner; the giggle of a child or the smile of his grandparent as they enjoy a moment together. Life provides joy daily if we're willing to see it. Can't find it in front of you? Search the internet for good stories. They're there (even if we have to search a little harder for them, thanks to a negatively-focused news culture). Find something that makes you laugh: a video, a song, or even better, a friend. Once you find something that works, focus completely on it. Turn the alerts off, ignore the clock, and spend just a few minutes mindfully enjoying the moment. You will find over time that you have less regrets about

GRATITUDE IS THE ANTIDOTE TO SUFFERING

life passing you by. You will also find it easier to identify what you are grateful for.

Mindfulness and Suffering

We do not usually think of gratitude and suffering together, but we should. Often what causes us pain, angst, and sorrow is evidence we loved, grew, and experienced life. These are gifts life gives us to become better versions of ourselves. Suffering is difficult and something most of us would rather not experience. If we can connect it to what we are grateful for, it helps us make sense of what we're experiencing. But more importantly, we can relieve some of our suffering by focusing on what we are grateful for.

During my time responding to the Joplin tornado, every victim (without exception) expressed deep and terrible suffering associated with this disaster. They were exhausted, sad, shocked, and terrified. They didn't know how they were going to rebuild their lives and grieved all they lost. But through gratitude they knew they *would* rebuild. They were able to intuitively connect what they had, versus what they didn't, to the process of rebuilding. Gratitude empowers us to place our suffering in context to the greater experience of life, linking our trials to our later successes.

If you are suffering, *lean into it*. Sit with it, allowing it to tell you what it needs. Suffering multiplies when we resist it. Embracing and appreciating it helps us overcome it. That's tough to hear because our inclination is to distract from, avoid, or mitigate our suffering until it is gone. (Psst: it doesn't go away. It will rear its ugly head when you least expect it until it is dealt with in a healthy way). Suffering is unpleasant, distracting, and potentially destructive. *It's also necessary to the human experience.* Leaning into your suffering may be impossible at first, depending on the experience, but eventually the time will come where it is possible. And when it is possible, embrace it. Acknowledge it for all it is: the feelings, the loss, the impact it has on your being. Ask what it is teaching you, telling you, or requiring of you. Acknowledge it with words: *this is tough. I don't want to feel this way. I hurt right now.* Mindfully acknowledging our suffering removes its power to subconsciously sabotage us. The stillness of mindfulness, the feeling of acceptance, is what you lean into to help you heal and move forward.

Suffering is evidence we have lived meaningfully and experienced life's inevitable changes. While it can't be avoided, both mindfulness and gratitude can help put it in perspective and make it useful to your future.

The Appreciation-Focused Mindset

The best way to practice gratitude on a regular basis is to develop an appreciation-focused mindset. This means you experience life through the filter of opportunity rather than deficit. It is sometimes difficult and counterintuitive to our more negatively focused human ways, but when done well, it leads to great solutions and creative living. Those with an appreciative mindset immediately identify what works rather than what doesn't, are able to motivate others to capitalize on their best qualities, and can quickly identify how to optimize less-than-perfect circumstances. People with this mindset immediately assess others for their strengths which helps them build stronger relationships. When you approach a new situation, ask yourself what is good about it: What opportunities are apparent? What can be learned? And, if possible, what fun can be found as a result of this challenge?

One of my closest friends and I have this mindset about travel. We have, more than once, been in crazy and difficult situations on the road including being locked out of lodging upon arrival (and, a different trip, at 2 a.m. in the snow…), being stuck in a hurricane, forgetting to make necessary arrangements for important things, medical emergencies (a result of swimming with dolphins), flat tires, canoe mishaps, horsefly attacks, and more. But you know what? We love traveling together! Because, while others around us did not always find it as amusing, each of these experiences created amazing memories for us. Our attitude about traveling together is, "what adventures will we find this time?" And that's a great way to experience various parts of the world. We have an appreciative approach to traveling together: no matter what we face, we know it'll at least be a great story to tell later.

This mindset applies to our work life, too. Leaders who express and practice gratitude are resilient, motivating, and effective. They use an appreciative approach to business, focusing on what works: processes that are effective; products that the company is good at making and selling rather than what failed in the market; and understanding what makes their team work well together vs. individually. It is the ability to say, "let's keep doing this," rather than "what's wrong?" Let me be clear: fixing problems is an innate part of any business. But those who can simultaneously focus on strengths choose the best solutions with the best outcome of supporting their teams.

During the pandemic and shutdowns, many businesses learned the importance of an appreciative approach to leadership. While flexibility was the quality in highest demand, an appreciative outlook was a close second. Leaders had to know what products and services would be needed and viable in a drastically different market. They had to know how to send teams home (or mitigate risks onsite) in ways that were minimally disruptive to business.

EXERCISE: 10 DAYS TO GRATITUDE: AN ACTION PLAN

Gratitude is a daily practice that requires focus and commitment. It includes dedicated time to specific methods such as journaling (and there are many helpful journals out there to get you started!), but it also can be integrated into daily activities with a little effort. The following is a guide to helping you practice gratitude more often and with better intent. **For the next 10 days**, commit to doing the following (using either the individual or team criteria):

Practices for Individuals

1. **Say thank you**. The most obvious, and least practiced, form of gratitude is simply thanking others for what you are grateful for. Until it becomes more engrained into your daily practice, commit to saying thank you at least five times a day over the 10 days. It can be for any reason: obvious ones like someone holding a door open for you or assisting you in some way, or something more concerted such as thanking someone for being a good friend. This process will get easier over time and you'll be surprised how often it feels natural to express gratitude.

2. **Practice LOVE.** Using the LOVE method (Look, Observe, Validate, Experience), journal or reflect upon what you are grateful for. Specifically spend time on the "look" and "observe" steps to increase the quantity and quality of your gratitude. Answer the following questions for 10 days:

   a. What new things did you notice today to be grateful for? Do you wish you would've noticed or appreciated any of them sooner?

   b. Where has your appreciation deepened (if it has)?

   c. What was difficult about finding things to be grateful for today? What negative thoughts, if any, did you struggle with?

3. **Alter your View.** Think of a challenge you are facing currently (it can be the same one for the 10 days of this challenge or different ones—it's up to you). Start with this thought: *This is a good thing, because....* Do you believe that? Why or why not? Focus on changing your viewpoint about the challenge. Ask yourself these questions:

   a. How can the challenge be seen for its growth, lessons, or solutions?

   b. What alternate mindset could I choose for this? (Even if you don't choose one of them, engage in the imaginative process of identifying alternate viewpoints).

    c.   What problems or challenges would you rather have than this one?

4. **Identify your Strengths.** Instead of focusing on what you lack, spend these 10 days identifying your strengths. Name at least one strength of character you are grateful for each day. Remember: strengths are usually the "flip side" of our weaknesses. If you are feeling down on yourself because you struggled to speak up assertively in a meeting, what strength did this exhibit? Likely you are a calming, mediative presence to those around you. Didn't check everything off your to-do list? That's because you prioritized being a good parent, spending more time with your child who needed more of your attention than usual. This exercise doesn't eliminate our shortcomings… it highlights our strengths, which are every bit as important as anything we may need to work on.

5. **Spread gratitude.** In addition to saying thank you, do one thing each day that shows gratitude to someone else. It can be as simple as a kind gesture, a little gift, telling someone what you appreciate about them, or offering to fill in for someone who wants to leave early. Whatever you do, do it without expectation of recognition or reciprocity. Gratitude, as a verb, is synonymous with service.

Practices for Teams

Similar to the individual practices, challenge your team to do the following for 10 days:

Group reflection. Designate a specific time (30-45 minutes) over the next 10 days with your team to focus on what has gone well, what works, and what your team has achieved in the recent past. This is a time only for gratitude—problems, unless appreciated for their solution or lessons learned, should be left aside. This is a time to be mindful about what is working well for your group.

1. **Focus on Strengths.** As a team, make a comprehensive list of the strengths the team collectively possesses. One or more team members can possess the strength; the point is to collectively "own" the strengths of the whole team. You may have someone on the team that is great at attention to detail, another that is creative, and another that is strategic: all three of these strengths should be included on the list. Keep the list visible for the team to see.

2. **Celebrate.** Whether it's a birthday, anniversary, milestone, project finished, someone's dog's gotcha day...it doesn't matter. Set aside a time to celebrate at least once during your 10-day challenge. Studies show that when groups celebrate together—when they are grateful for a shared purpose—morale lifts and productivity rises.

3. **Encourage questions.** Inquiry is appreciative by nature. For the 10 days of this challenge, encourage more questions to be asked in meetings, discussions, and planning

activities. Instead of solution-seeking, only ask questions and don't worry if you don't have the answers to them for the 10 days of the exercise. You'll find after the 10 days that you have opened new lines of thinking and solution-mining just by asking the questions. You will be grateful for the results!

4. ***Extra credit:*** if you want to really challenge your team, ask them to conduct what I call a "Questionstorming" session. Just like a brainstorming session, the participants are only allowed to ask questions—any question, regardless of how "silly" it seems—and the questions are documented. At a later time, if you choose, you can select questions to seek answers for. It is a great way to get your team's creativity flowing!

Gratitude is a Choice

However you decide to begin your journey towards grateful living, remember that it is a choice you must make often and consistently. Your mind will argue with you in the beginning, resisting the urge to let go of its negative bent. It may seem strange or even silly at first to think in a more appreciative way (I admit to a few eye rolls myself when I started this process!). But over time you will notice that you see circumstances differently and experience life in a more vibrant way. Eventually you will build your resilience muscles with information, examples, and feelings of gratitude that help you relieve stress and increase problem-solving during difficult times.

THE FLEXIBLE OWN THE FUTURE

A tree that cannot bend will crack in the wind. The hard and stiff will be broken; the soft and supple will prevail.

—Lao Tzu

The Space Between

"The space between what is, and what you believe should be, is the amount of suffering you'll experience."

A room full of leaders stared at me. This was a consultation on change management; what was I talking about? I repeated the statement and paused. I watched as some participants' eyes widened with understanding, while others furrowed their brows. A woman spoke up tentatively.

"So, what you're saying is, we haven't *accepted* this acquisition?"

"Exactly," I smiled. "Your struggle isn't about the acquisition. You've all recognized the benefits of this change and you've agreed unanimously to it. You're resisting change itself. This is about letting go of expectations, comfort, identity, and desires. In other words, this is a problem of leadership's flexibility. And your success is defined directly by how flexible you are willing to be."

I let this sink in over a quick break. I was working with a group of leaders who had just undergone the loss of their small, local nonprofit to a larger, national conglomerate. While they were nostalgic about their role in their community for the past 50 years, they understood that this move was financially and strategically sound. They knew the services they provided would have a much greater impact under the well-funded and established parent company than standing alone. But every step of the way the staff—and much of the leadership—resisted the changes brought on by this acquisition, whether it was the new software programs, different leadership styles, new services, or staffing structure changes. Days were spent lamenting and complaining rather than acclimating to the new operational standards. No one seemed incapable of these changes; rather, they seemed unwilling. Every part of the acquisition seemed painful and took longer than leadership thought it should.

When everyone returned from break, I asked their thoughts about what I had suggested. Could it be that they were resisting change itself? Most nodded. One man looked upset.

"Would you mind sharing what you're thinking?" I asked him.

He paused for a moment, folded his arms over his chest, and said, "I hadn't thought about this until now. Our organization has never been good at change. We drive home the need for consistency in every process, every task. Some of our processes haven't changed since our founding. I've been here 20 years, and I've never seen anyone challenge the status quo effectively."

I thanked him for his honesty and vulnerability and asked the remaining leaders what they thought. Did they agree that change was generally discouraged in the organization? If so, what impact did this have on their staff and services? What was their outlook on creativity and innovation? And finally, what attitudes or cultural practices needed to shift to be successful in the future?

They had a lengthy discussion about the culture of their organization regarding change. While they discussed, I documented their key findings:

- *Change is discouraged because it disrupts well-functioning systems.*
- *Innovation is at best ignored, and at worst discouraged.*
- *Some leaders believe change means admitting they were somehow wrong before.*

- *Change is scary: what if we don't like the new way of doing things? What if we fail?*

I took some time to process this with the group, helping them discover how to move forward effectively. As a change management consultant, I have worked with many clients stuck in one of what I call the **"5D"** phases of emotional response to change:

Phase One: Denial

Ignorance is bliss! In this stage we simply ignore the change is happening. Perhaps it hasn't happened yet, hasn't affected us yet, or we don't want to think about it because it's unpleasant. We may not believe the change is coming because we've heard it all before or because we don't think it's achievable. Whatever the reason, it hasn't sunk in yet that the change is real and imminent.

Phase Two: Defiance

We realize the change is real and our inner two-year-old kicks in. In this stage we resist the impending change. We stand our ground, make noise, and insist we're not going to be a part of it (in its milder forms, this often manifests as refusal to learn a new system, behavior, or process). We know the change is coming (no more denying it), but we don't have to go along with it!

Phase Three: Denouncement

Okay, okay, the change is coming. We might not be able to stop it, and someone might be able to make us do something different, but we can sure say something about it! Here's where we vocally object to change: it's the wrong move, we'll fail, no one is listening, "they" just want to assert their power, what we're doing now works fine, and so on. Though usually short-lived, a lot of damage can occur to morale in this stage as we affect others with our negativity. *Note: For those who go through this stage quietly, it is conveyed in facial expressions or passive-aggressive behaviors, felt as helplessness, or experienced as complacency.*

Phase Four: Decompression

Ah, relief! We're starting to see that while we're powerless over the change, we have a powerful choice in how we adjust to it. If we're lucky, we recognize that the change may even be for the best. We may still be somewhat reluctant in this stage, but we're lessening our negativity and begin behaving in ways that accept or support the change.

Phase Five: Demonstration

In this stage we've reached commitment and are demonstrating the change (through observable behavior) that we've been asked to make. We may still doubt or dislike it from time to time, but overall, we've embraced it and are practicing it as our "new normal." In its best version, we even express our appreciation for the change. Either way, we are now onboard and intend to make it successful.

When I see a group stuck in one of these phases (this group was in late Phase 3), I know that either (1) the timing is off, or (2) the culture is off. When a change is demanded too quickly (an unexpected merger, for example) or too abruptly (such as a crisis), our minds do not adjust properly to the new demands. We may be capable of doing them—as demonstrated by the incredibly quick adjustments communities, families, and companies made during the pandemic—but that doesn't mean our minds are up-to-speed. (In fact, if you look at how the world adjusted to the pandemic, we were quick to adjust *behaviorally* to new practices, but experienced record burnout, resignations, divorces, and mental health crises). Our minds must have appropriate time to process new information and make meaningful connections to a desired change.

But if enough time has passed, we've done the hard work of adjusting our mind and habits to change, and we're still stuck, it's a reflection of culture. It means we (as an individual or group) have come to believe that change itself is negative, scary, or inappropriate. Perhaps we don't have experience making significant changes, have created a culture that supports consistency above innovation, or must adhere to rigid guidelines due to the nature of our work. Whatever the reason, we have created a belief that change should be shunned or resisted. And this is when we lose our resilience.

Simply put, **you are only as resilient as you are flexible**. Change is inevitable. The past is permanent; the future is mailable. Change happens whether we like it (or not), want it (or not), or care about the outcome (or not). Resilient people don't waste time resisting change. They anticipate it, embrace it, and figure out quickly how they're going to adjust to it. They get to work: they acknowledge and overcome fears associated with the change, they are self-aware of how the change affects them (where they are in the 5D Phases), they choose a positive mindset regarding the change, they are grateful for the opportunities the change may bring, they see the inherent possibilities in the change, and they have the confidence that they will be able to successfully adapt to the change. In other words, they engage all the principles of resilience in order to increase their flexibility and guarantee successful adjustment to the change.

Radical Acceptance

If the amount of space between what is, and what you believe should be, is the amount of suffering you'll experience, how do we close the gap? Through **radical acceptance**. Radical acceptance requires us to let go of what we thought something (or someone) was, what it could be, and what we want it to be. It requires us to *accept solely and completely what is*. When we radically accept something, we stop fighting against it. We surrender to reality. We stop suffering because we realize to do so is futile. Instead, we turn our attention to what we will do now: how our life will go on, how we will find new opportunities, and which path we will forge as a result of our circumstances. It's not easy, and it's not for the faint of heart. And it is necessary if we are to be truly resilient.

Radical acceptance focuses mindfully on the present. It says, "I can do this *right now*." "I can survive this." "I can't change the past, but I can accept what has happened if *even just for today*." Paradoxically, as you sit with what *is* in the current moment, your mind will start to feel the gap close between what has been and what could be. You will feel more clarity about the effects of your circumstances on the greater whole of your life: that what you're experiencing, feeling, or doing is temporary. And as you gain acceptance of your circumstances, thoughts, and emotions, you will find flexibility comes naturally.

Occasionally we fail to accept our circumstances (or an imminent change) because to do so is to let ourselves down. It is, in a sense, accepting what we deem unacceptable. It's important to remember in those moments that acceptance is not the same as defeat. It is not the same as complacency. And it does not ask us to give up perseverance. It is simply asking that we accept reality in this moment, *if only for this moment*. It allows us the opportunity to choose our reaction and plan our success based on reliable information: the facts.

Though much of my work focuses on businesses who are dealing with external circumstances they must accept, I also encourage leaders to engage in radical *self*-acceptance. Using the same premise as radical acceptance, radical self-acceptance means acknowledging who you are—warts and all—for the present moment. It requires us to be fully responsible for all we are, all we do, and all we think. It is not giving into the myth of "not good enough" or other forms of lack. To the contrary, it positively accepts who we are fully and unconditionally in the present moment. It says, "I am ok; I'm still learning." "I accept that I behaved in a way that was less than ideal, and that I can change that in the future." And "I take responsibility for all I do, both my failures and my successes." When we make a conscious effort to think this way, we release judgement of ourselves and are able to determine more authentically who we want to be. This reality-based thinking leads us to better flexibility and resilience.

EXERCISE: RADICAL ACCEPTANCE

Think of a circumstance in your life that you wish was different. Perhaps it's a friendship that isn't working, a promotion you didn't get, or a skill you haven't mastered. Now answer the following questions:

1. What is the reality of this situation? What can't I change?
2. What is my present state? What do I feel about this? *Be specific: what do you feel in your body? What thoughts do you have? What do you feel emotionally?*
3. What does it mean to accept this situation? What judgement(s) do I need to release?
4. Do I radically accept myself? Why or why not?

Your Personal Mission

David H. McConnell was a door-to-door book salesman in the late 1800s[6] when he noticed that his female customers weren't as interested in the books as the free samples of perfume that came with them. He decided that, rather than continue trying to sell books, he could sell perfume. And to reach more women, he recruited women to sell at a time when many women didn't have career opportunities. His innovative gambles paid off: he became the founder of Avon, which amasses over $9 billion annually in global sales more than a century later.

What if McConnell had continued to sell books? He was a book salesman. That's what he did; that's the business he was in. Companies make this mistake all the time: regardless of market opportunity, they stick to what they went into business to do and, worse, commit to the only way they do it. They refuse to be flexible. McConnell realized his *why*—to sell products people want or need—was more important than his *how*.

---

6 *Wikipedia contributors. In Wikipedia, The Free Encyclopedia. Retrieved May 28, 2022. https://en.wikipedia.org/wiki/Avon_Products*

Knowing how, and when, to pivot is key to running a successful business. During the pandemic, thousands of businesses survived because they knew how to be flexible. They were not wedded to the specific method of providing their product or service. Instead, they created ways to continue their mission (the *why* of their business) while being flexible with the *how*. Some developed ways to put in-person services online. Some moved from stationary products (such as restaurants) to carry-out or delivery versions. And many developed new product lines altogether, such as the large number of distilleries who created much-needed hand sanitizer for their communities. While many businesses unfortunately shuttered, far more stayed afloat through creativity and flexibility.

I'm not saying this is an easy process—ask any business owner or leader how they feel coming out of the pandemic. We are collectively exhausted, winded from a continuous series of blows to our operations, and in some cases financially drained. But we made it. We acted on our why and did what was necessary to keep moving. That's what's important, and what we will build upon to manage the next adversity that comes our way.

This is true of our personal lives, too: if we know our *why*, it's much easier to be flexible with our how, when, and where. What motivates you the most? Likely it's your partner, children, community, or passion. It's your mission, your values, your commitments. The irrefutable and nonnegotiable things that make you, *you*. Your why should lead all else: how you behave, who you surround yourself with, and the choices you make.

In the late 90s I attended a seminar on personal mission statements. Though I thought it sounded lofty, my boss thought we would all benefit from thinking about our personal "whys." We were asked to come to the seminar with a list of our favorite verbs. My list included words like create, inspire, hope, achieve, influence, write, sing, and spark. My colleagues' lists were quite different: calm, persuade, work, run, sleep, contextualize, love, hug, remember. These lists were an interesting reflection of our values and personalities.

We were then asked to write down what was most important to us on a personal level: what were our most deeply held beliefs? What impact did we want to leave on humanity? How would we know if we lived a successful life? What would be our greatest achievement during our time on Earth? (I was right; this was lofty!).

Of our answers to these questions, the facilitator asked us to choose two to work with to create our mission statements. I struggled to even identify one—it seemed like such an arduous task to write down the contribution I wanted to make to humanity! Noticing my frustration, the facilitator stopped by my seat to offer help.

"What is your favorite feeling?" she asked. "What gives you goose bumps, and always leaves you feeling on top of the world? Write that down."

I thought for a bit, then realized that what I love, more than anything, is watching someone realize they are more capable than they previously believed. I don't watch the Olympics for the sports (I enjoy only a few of those). I watch religiously for two weeks to see the medal moments, the underdog wins, the surprise knockout achievements. My favorite books and movies are those that tell stories of triumph over unbelievable odds—I can't get enough of them. In other words, what I love most is *the human spirit exceeding itself.*

I wrote, "I want to witness the human spirit exceeding itself," and realized I had quite a passive mission statement. Just as I was imagining my life as some sort of achievement groupie going from sporting events to spelling bees with a cooler and lawn chair in tow, the facilitator asked us to choose 3-4 verbs from our list. These would become the foundation of our personal mission statement: what we will *do* in the world. We were asked to craft a short, 3-verbed sentence that encapsulated our mission.

By the end of the afternoon, I had written the simple phrase, "hope, inspire, and seek the extraordinary." For me, hope is verb—a powerful one. It is a way of living, a call to resilience. To inspire others—particularly to help them discover they are capable of more than they dreamed—is my pinnacle idea of personal achievement. Seeking the extraordinary? That's equal parts my desire to live adventurously and my love of the magical moments life has to offer.

Here's the amazing thing about completing this exercise so many years ago: I wouldn't change a word. I still have that mission displayed in my office, and I still try to live up to it every day. My *why* frames everything I do and every relationship that's important to me. But even more amazing? I can be entirely flexible within my mission. How I achieve this day-to-day ranges widely, but I try to go to bed each night having hoped for a better world, attempting to inspire someone to think more greatly about themselves and their circumstances, and having appreciated some tiny magic in an otherwise ordinary day. It doesn't matter how I do it, where I do it, or when I do it. It matters that I do it.

This is how flexibility works in resilience, too. Know *why* you want to do something, why it matters to you and your loved ones, and why it will matter 10 years from now. If it won't matter 10 minutes, 10 days, or 10 years from now, eliminate your worry and stress about it! If what you want more than anything is for your children to know they were fully loved, for example, the difficulties and challenges you face won't matter as much as what you did to love them through those difficulties. If making a difference in a specific community or cause is your mission, how you do it is up to you. It's flexible. Because you can make as much of a difference helping one person as a thousand.

When times get tough, resilient people get going—and they don't stop to worry about whether it's the right way to do it. They just *do* for what they believe in.

EXERCISE: YOUR PERSONAL WHY

Similar to writing a personal mission statement, reflect on the following questions to help determine your "why:"

1. Who are the most important people in your life?
2. What impression of you do you want to leave with someone you meet?
3. What impact do you hope to make in your community? Why is this important to you?
4. If you had 3 months to live, what would be nonnegotiable to accomplish?

5. If you have five hundred years to live, what would be nonnegotiable to accomplish?

Breakdown to Breakthrough

As you probably know, men and women who join the U.S. military are required to go through Basic Training. Most of us, even those who have not served, have heard how rigorous and stressful these weeks can be. Participants are pushed physically, mentally, and emotionally. They lose their sense of autonomy and self-image. Ego quickly takes a back seat to obedience. This process can be grueling, terrifying, and exhilarating. While they lose their sense of self momentarily, they gain an understanding of a wider range of personal capabilities. They rebuild a better version of themselves as they learn new skills and strategies. They are, in essence, broken down in order to break through. So successful is this effort that civilian programs have sprung up to do the same. Programs, camps, and trainers push people to their limits in order to help them realize their full potential. This is exactly how it works when we face adversity.

When things are tough, our emotions can make us think we're failing at resilience. Circumstances push us to our limits, and we succumb to self-doubt and pity. It's disorienting when we engage in behaviors we don't recognize in ourselves or lose sight of who we thought we were. Little moments seem catastrophic as we cry over the proverbial milk. Choose to think of these moments differently: **life sometimes asks us to breakdown to breakthrough**.

Most of the people I know who have successfully overcome significant adversities wouldn't have chosen these experiences, but feel they are better for them. When the dust settled, they realized they emerged a better version of themselves. They now possessed new skills, wisdom, or strength they hadn't previously. Many report a changed outlook, better relationships, and a deeper enjoyment of life. While the event or circumstances were unwanted and painful, the outcome is like a butterfly emerging from the cocoon.

This is the Breakdown to Breakthrough effect: life gives us circumstances that require us to release what doesn't work, change what is ineffective, and stop what is harmful. We shed a part of our former self to make room for a new and better version. Sometimes we grieve what we are losing, other times letting go is easy. But it always requires flexibility. If we resist this kind of change, we fall prey to stagnation and eventual depression. Embracing our break- throughs requires us to accept what we can't change, change what we can, and be optimistic about what is to come. That's flex- ibility in action.

The good news is that people are more resilient than they realize. We thrive after our breakthroughs. You possess many of the qualities and skills to get through life's toughest challenges, even when you fear you don't. It's only when we're tested that we fully understand what we're capable of, and most of us are capable of far more than we suspected. If you're going through a breakdown, hang on...the breakthrough coming will be well worth it.

Would You Rather?

Would You Rather? is one of my favorite icebreakers and games. It goes like this: would you rather spend 20 years alone on a deserted island or with ten people you don't like? Would you rather be known as smart or nice? Would you rather be trapped with a lion for an hour or a week with your in-laws? (Don't ask this one at Thanksgiving.)

This game is fun and insightful. But more importantly, it makes us think about the choices we make. When our minds are forced to choose, we find out how flexible—or inflexible—we really are. Crisis, stress, and challenges often come with limited choices. But that doesn't mean we can't solve our problems—and complete our mission—within those choices. Our power lies in activating our choices. It lies in flexibly embracing whatever comes our way.

Think about the following "would you rather" questions. There are no wrong answers; these are simply to get you thinking about how you might be flexible when times are difficult. If you are faced with a difficult decision or circumstances, what's the opposite? What would you rather be stuck with?

1. Would you rather live without love, or without fear?
2. Would you rather be seen as difficult to deal with, or easy to manipulate?
3. Would you rather rely on an imperfect friend or a perfect stranger?
4. Would you rather be paid less but have autonomy, or be paid more and be micromanaged?
5. Would you rather lose everything but have your integrity, or keep everything but have to lie and cheat?

Life is hard. Really hard. It often gives us limited options…but there is always a choice. You can stay down or get up. You can give in or get going. Resilience requires us to be flexible enough to accept the choices available. Resilient people don't obsess over unavailable options or ideals. They simply act upon the best choice available to them.

Everyone is capable of flexible thinking and response. The first step towards resilience is accepting the circumstances of your life. If they can be changed, outline an action plan for how you will make the change happen. If they can't be changed, how will you adjust? What options are available to you? Make a new plan with this in mind. Most importantly, let go of what can't be changed. Of what can never be. However possible, use the circumstances available to you to your advantage. **Live into what is possible.**

Parents of special needs children understand too well what it feels like to reconstruct their hopes and ideals for their child. The flexibility required of these parents is extraordinary. They must accept that their child will have a radically different life than the one they anticipated, with challenges and heartache they didn't expect. And they have to rebuild their lives around the needs of this child. From limited options they make exceptional choices: to work with their child to maximize their potential; to rally resources to support the family and the child so they can adapt their daily living to the needs of the child; to learn about their child's condition and meet with other families experiencing similar challenges; to work with medical professionals to give their child the best opportunities for a healthy outcome.

Several children in my family have special needs, including autism, developmental delay, Prader Willi Syndrome (find out more and support families at pwsausa.org), and difficult dietary restrictions. The daily struggles for my family members are sometimes overwhelming, but these kids are among the greatest, smartest, kindest, and most beautiful souls I know. They have learned to adjust their lives in creative and exemplary ways to be able to keep up with their classmates. Their parents adjust their lives to give them the best opportunities possible, and as a result these children are happy and well-loved. Being around them is a constant and beautiful reminder of what it is to be resilient.

Since the onset of the pandemic, I have worked with several companies on resilient strategies for making it through this difficult time. Some of these companies were quick to accept what was happening and needed to be done; others struggled significantly. All my clients made it through, but those who were flexible with their products, services, or operating style (i.e., working remotely or in varying shifts) were more productive, had lower turnover, and emerged with a better bottom line. Some have permanently shifted the way they do business, offering more remote and digital products and services. Those who simply "rode out" the time, making very few changes to their operating or output, are now struggling to overcome stagnation, resignations, and financial depression. As difficult as it has been to witness, it is a stark reminder that our ability to be flexible to life's demands and circumstances is essential to our resilience.

For Reflection

Answer the following questions to challenge your flexible thinking:

1. What can't I control about my current circumstances? What can I control? *More importantly, what can I control that I might be missing or denying?*
2. How would my outlook shift if I radically accepted my circumstances?
3. Does it scare me to take more responsibility for my circumstances, accepting and controlling all that I can? If so, what scares me about it?

What is one thing I can do today—*just for today*—to make my life better?

PRINCIPLE SIX:

YOUR PURPOSE IS TO SERVE OTHERS

The best way to find yourself is to lose yourself in the service of others.

—Mahatma Gandhi

Going to the Bookstore

I love books. Not just the ideas or stories within them, but the *actual* books. The heft, the sounds of the spine crackling, the turning of pages. Among my favorite places are bookstores and libraries where I can scan titles for cleverness, flip through a potential find, and look for new resources. Sure, I own several books electronically for their portability and convenience. But I still love the bricks-and-mortar experience of seeing hundreds of titles and topics at my fingertips.

Sometime in my twenties, I noticed that I always went first to one of two areas of a bookstore: leadership (often via the business section) and self-help. I was neither a leader (at the time) nor a therapist, so I couldn't quite explain why this was. It was just what I was interested in; topics I never seemed to get bored learning or discussing. Several years later, as I was training a women's leadership program, a participant first asked what I have now been asked countless times in my work: "how do I know what my purpose is? How do I know what I'm *supposed* to be doing?"

I thought for a moment, then asked, "where do you go first in a bookstore?"

"Potty training," she said, as we all laughed.

But my question made its point: where we go first in a bookstore, what we search most online, and what we never tire of talking about is intrinsically linked to our purpose. I have always gravitated to subjects of leadership and of self-improvement—specifically resilience, though that specialization came later—because it is tied to my purpose. I never get tired of thinking about it, talking about it, or writing about it. It's what I would do even if I weren't paid to do it. And that's how I know it's how I am meant to help others.

This question of "purpose" seems to be gaining popularity in recent years. Younger generations want to feel connected to their work, to feel a sense of purpose. They are far more interested than previous generations in companies that have a strong social contribution. They don't just want a paycheck; they want to do work that matters. I've noticed this among middle-aged people, too: they are either done raising their kids and looking for a more fulfilling career, or they are nearing retirement but have no desire to slow down. As they approach life shifts, their thinking shifts to more meaningful work.

The problem with this question is that it is narrow in scope. It supposes that we are here to do only one thing, for one company or cause, or with one group of people. That's not how our purpose works. If it did, we'd certainly get bored or, worse, fail to have purpose when the company or cause ceased to exist. Resilience is more likely when we feel a sense of purpose in our life but finding it shouldn't pinhole us into limitations. It's wide open to possibilities.

What you do is up to you: it depends on the topics or people that light your fire, the thing you never tire of thinking about or doing. *How* you do it is also your choice: through your job, through volunteer work, or through roles like parent, teacher, and friend. But your purpose is to serve others. How do I know? Because we're wired this way. *Our happiness depends upon it.*

Studies have shown that connectivity with others, and specifically *doing* for others, lights up the same areas of our brain as rewards such as food and money. In one study, scientists utilized functional magnetic resonance imaging (fMRI) to investigate whether there is a link between generosity and happiness. Over a four-week experiment, they found it: spending money on others predicted an increase in happiness (and did so across ages and cultures).[7] And according to the 2022 World Happiness Report, benevolence (specifically donating, volunteering, and helping strangers) increased remarkably in 2021 in every global region (up almost 25% of its pre-pandemic level).[8] In most studies, nothing was more clearly and intrinsically linked to happiness than our connectivity (and service) to others.

Our resilience and longevity are also tied to how we relate to and serve others. We are not only programmed for connectedness, but we define ourselves by the roles we play in others' lives. "Empty nesters" often experience a sense of loss and depression because their children are no longer reliant upon them for their well-being. Until they find new ways to connect or contribute, retirees experience a similar sense of loss or depression because they are no longer connected to others through their work. Programs that unite elderly with youth have proven to increase the longevity of the elderly participants. We are meant to be connected in meaningful ways to others.

It makes sense, then, that our resilience—our ability to withstand life's most difficult challenges—is also reliant upon

7   Park, Kahnt, Dogan, Strang, Fehr, & Tobler, "A neural link between generosity and happiness," *Nature Communications*, 8, Article number: 15964 (2017). *https://www.nature.com/articles/ncomms15964*

8   Helliwell, John F., Layard, Richard, Sachs, Jeffrey D., De Neve, Jan-Emmanuel, Aknin, Lara B., Wang, Shun. *World Happiness Report Report 2022. World Happiness Report, https://world-happiness.report/ed/2022*

our connection to others. Over the past 15 years, I have asked hundreds of people how they successfully overcame specific, difficult challenges. Each time, community (family, friends, coworkers, or a chosen group) was among the top three answers, followed by hope and self-confidence. Many said things like, "I don't know what I'd have done without my family," "my faith community really came through for me," or "I'm so glad I work for a company that allowed me to do what I needed during that time…" Whatever the challenge, the solution is almost never accomplished alone.

We are more likely to deal positively with challenges if others depend on us to do so. And we're significantly more likely to overcome those challenges if we have a supportive, trusted network of people we can lean on. When a crisis or tragedy occurs, people gravitate towards each other. We hold vigils, ceremonies, and get-togethers to help others or to grieve with them. We don't want to experience our tragedies or triumphs alone. That's our nature. When we surround ourselves with a strong network of people who want what's best for us and are willing to help us, we are far more likely to emerge from adversity with the ability to thrive.

It doesn't matter if we're strangers or friends, these benefits work as long as the connection is authentic. For the first time in human history, we can connect to thousands of people anytime, anywhere, digitally. But this kind of connection is inauthentic. Using social media, we discuss deep and complex issues with people we don't know or have any emotional responsibility to, then wonder why our "relationships" feel shallow and judgmental. We email or text what could be spoken, then wonder why we are misunderstood. Companies replace customer service representatives with a computer or chat function, then wonder why customers are no longer loyal. Resilient relationships are built over time and with intimate knowledge of each other's thoughts, feelings, and characteristics. They are built, most importantly, on empathy. Empathy and authenticity aren't always possible through social media, texting, or digital communication. We need to see and hear each other when it matters most.

Just to be clear, I am a fan of remote working and believe most companies have a great opportunity to provide employees more flexibility through virtual and hybrid environments. But when it matters, such as when there is a problem or someone needs support, we must connect authentically. Pick up the phone. *See* each other on a screen. Or even better, meet in person. We are not wired to have wired relationships!

Community Responsibility

After my own experience as a victim of violence, I struggled to overcome a multitude of challenges alone: healing physically and emotionally, moving, finding a new job, paying significant medical bills. I didn't want to lean on others, burden anyone, or appear weak to those around me. That was a mistake. It was *not* resilient of me. I soon learned I could do very little to overcome such a significant obstacle alone. And I learned shortly after that that I didn't want to. It not only helped to have family and friends to help me, it was necessary. I needed support, love, and the help of mental health professionals. I needed my community. I don't think I began any real healing until I started going out with friends, attending church, talking to a therapist, spending time with family…whatever got me out of my apartment and away from my isolated misery. Experiencing grief alone is like screaming into an echo chamber, the grief bouncing back against you over and over with nothing to absorb it. We need others to help absorb and silence our pain.

Many of you know the adage, "God doesn't give us anything I can't handle." But He does. There are circumstances people face that lead them to incredibly debilitating depression, breakdowns, and even suicide. But here's what God (or life) doesn't do: give us anything we can't handle *without the help we need*. If we choose to look to others, we find the resources, support, and love we need to overcome our worst circumstances.

Not long after I got back on my feet, I started looking outward rather than inward. What could I do to help others in my situation? Was that my place, my calling? What difference could I make? These are questions we often ask ourselves after being touched by significant adversity such as a life-threatening disease, a child with special needs, or a natural disaster. Our minds want to make sense of our experience not just for us, but for others. We begin to think, "could I help others in my situation?" "Can I prevent others from going through what I just experienced?" We want our tragedies to serve a purpose. Sometimes life provides a way to do that; other times, it requires us to simply move on. You'll know when you feel the calling which is true for you. Either way, in all adversity, our impulse is to utilize and help our community. Something within not only recognizes we have a responsibility to others, but that we have a responsibility to *ourselves* to be a connected member of our society.

In my case, I first volunteered for organizations working on various issues of criminal justice. I used these opportunities to help mitigate my need to "make sense" of my experience. This led to my position working for several years with victims, serving as a local and national spokesperson for the myriad of effects crime and violence have on its victims.

Like many social issues, crime is often compounded by other factors such as poverty, social unrest, or educational inequity. I live approximately four miles from Ferguson, Missouri, where Michael Brown was shot and killed in 2014. His death ignited a global uprising and conversation about racial injustice and police brutality. Much of my work before that time involved working with community leaders and media to recognize the impact of crime on victims, including advocating for those whose cases are over-looked due to racial or economic status. After Michael Brown's death, I was asked to help with community conversations regarding race and policing. This was, and remains, the most difficult work of my life. I went on to work with the Supreme Court of Missouri on criminal justice reform and to help several companies hold critical conversations about equity in the workplace. Throughout all the conversations, panels, town hall meetings, training sessions, medi-ations, legislative witnessing, and media interviews, one thought remained consistent in my mind: community undeniably impacts our resilience. It can build us up or tear us down. Our ability to feel like we belong is imperative to overcoming social obstacles bigger than ourselves. When we don't feel we belong we whither, failing to reach our full potential. This is true in neighborhoods, schools, workplaces—anywhere groups gather. If we want a better world, a world resilient against adversity, we must care deeply about all the people who are in it.

In today's digital and busy world, we are failing to make these necessary connections to each other. We don't know our neighbors anymore. We don't care about the people we pass on the street; we are looking at our phones instead of making eye contact with the world. We are too busy to ask colleagues how they are or what they are experiencing day-to-day. When someone is struggling, we assume it is someone else's problem to fix.

This collective apathy is taking a sad and lasting toll on humanity. Our communities are plagued by mental health crises, poverty, crime, hunger, and drug addiction. We look to politicians or corporations to fix the problem, unwilling to seek solutions for ourselves. Resilient communities and organizations know that *every* person—without exception—is responsible for the strength of the whole. Each individual's challenges weigh on our collective wellness. Our communities, and our companies, must decide that the wellbeing of all its members is paramount to its success. This doesn't mean we always have to do *for* others (in fact, to do so is to rob them of the pride and resilience of helping themselves). But we must be willing to meet others where they are, connect them with resources to help themselves, and support them through challenges. This might look like establishing employee assistance and wellbeing programs in our organizations, providing better free mental health services and centers in our communities, or empowering families to provide or secure onsite, ongoing assistance for their elderly family members. It looks like having the knowledge of what challenges our community members face and the perseverance to help solve these challenges.

This isn't always easy, particularly when addressing systems and relationships that have been harmful to a particular individual or group. Mediation and reparation may be necessary. Systems must be challenged and changed, if necessary, to accommodate the needs of all that utilize them. For example, many places across the United States still do not meet the needs of wheelchair-bound individuals, despite laws requiring accessibility. These individuals, whose lives are already difficult in ways that most others cannot relate to, are left more isolated as a result. We do not always think of what we don't directly experience, to our collective peril.

The Workplace Community

Leaders tend to think they must employ one-size-fits-all solutions to problems in respect to fairness. This often leaves employees feeling resentful and unrecognized. Employees are motivated by a variety of factors, face differing challenges, and have different stressors based on their role in the organization. Recognizing their efforts and meeting their needs requires flexibility from leaders. It requires us to listen intently for what matters to individuals and provide support and resources that, to the best of our ability and efficiency, meet their individual needs.

A friend of mine used to work for a small manufacturer whose day shift started at 7:30 am. Most of their employees are line workers, receiving salaries not much higher than minimum wage. A few years ago, leaders in the company began noticing that a handful of employees were chronically late. Not by much—often 10 to 15 minutes—but it was a problem, nonetheless. The leaders first gave verbal warnings. Then written notices. Then they fired employees.

But when they hired new employees, the same thing happened. The employees offered explanations, but the leaders heard them as excuses. They just assumed they were in a business and pay range that attracted people with poor work ethic. They told employees that if they couldn't be on time, this may not be the job for them.

Then a good friend of mine was hired into the company in a senior Human Resources position. Tired of processing dismissal paperwork merely weeks after hiring, she sat down with four of the offending employees.

"You're not in trouble," she explained to them. "I know you've been spoken to about this, but nothing has changed. I just really need to understand what is causing you to be late."

One young woman explained that the school buses in her neighborhood come at 6:50, and she's a single mom of small children. There was no one to get the kids on the bus if she left any earlier. A man nodded that he, too, had a similar situation with the bus that picks up his elderly mother for an adult daycare program.

That accounted for two employees, but nine more employees on the day shift were late on a regular basis. What was going on? In speaking with a few more employees, my friend found the culprit: public transit. Many of their employees relied upon buses to get to work in a town where public transportation was scarce. The employees who were chronically late lived predominantly in one area of the town, an area with limited access to frequent buses. The timing of the best route put their arrival around 7:40 am.

My friend took this finding to leadership. Upon realizing the issue, they were upset by the number of workers they had let go in the previous year. The company shifted its start time to 7:45, and now makes small allowances for occasional lateness.

What happened in my friend's company is unfortunately not rare. Companies frequently miss systemic, community problems affecting the productivity of their employees. Recognizing the unique needs of specific groups, some legislators have taken action to mandate specific accommodations (such as mother's rooms) in the workplace. But waiting for the government to mandate an action that would assist many employees doesn't build morale. Willingly and proactively recognizing the work community does. If leaders take the time to really listen to what is affecting their workforce and make reasonable adjustments to accommodate, they'll find it much easier to retain good talent.

Work/Life Integration

One of the most common questions I am asked when I speak with women's groups is, "how can I achieve better work/life balance?" (As our culture balances family roles better, men are beginning to ask this question more often, too.) Here's my answer: there's no such thing anymore. There is work/life *integration*. This doesn't mean we can't—or shouldn't—unplug from work (we can and must). Rather, it's a reflection of the digitization of our world and more people in the workplace. It's simply what happens in today's world. We can no longer keep work and home lives completely separate when both parents or single parents are working: homes still need caring for, children still have medical appointments during the workday, our cars still have to be serviced. Our personal lives don't only happen after 5 pm and on weekends. So, we've integrated them into our workday, and our workday into our off time. We check email after the kids go to bed. We answer a quick business call on the weekend. We talk to our child's teacher while we're at work. We make both worlds work because we must. This balancing act is a great example of resilience: our society has begun creating systems and practices that support this juggling act of work and home. It has to if we're to be productive and well. We bend to the demands of what's important, such as work and family. But how well we do that is up to us.

If you are a leader, take a moment to think about the policies and practices that enable your employees to do their best work while also being their best selves. Do you support their ability to take off a few minutes early to attend their child's game or teacher conference? Do you allow flexibility for personal medical appointments? If your workplace is structured onsite and with inflexible schedules (such as manufacturing or retail), do you have ample personal time policies? How well you support those who work for and with you will have a direct impact on the resilience of your workplace.

Connectedness and Health

Studies show that people with strong relationships, specifically with family, friends, and community, increases our wellness, cognitive health, and longevity. One study, which included data from more than 309,000 people, discovered that when people lacked strong relationships their risk of premature death rose by 50%, a risk greater than obesity.[9] Similarly, scientists are currently discovering a link between healthy relationships and lower dementia in the elderly. It's not the number of relationships, necessarily, but the quality of those relationships that improves our outlook, immunity, and wellbeing. We need others to stimulate our thoughts and emotions and create a sense of purpose in our lives. Wellness rarely happens in a vacuum: we need the joy and love of connecting to others to thrive.

Conversely, when community members around us ail, so do we. Several community health models indicate that the behaviors and conditions of our environment, often defined by our culture, affect our personal wellness. For example, our eating, sleeping, working, personal hygiene, and mental health habits are intrinsically linked to those of the people around us. If the people in our family or community don't trust doctors, we don't tend to go to the doctor as often. If our spouse is eats unhealthily, we tend to have a harder time losing weight. When organizations are dedicated to healthy living—having access for employees to healthy snacks, for example—the workforce behaves in healthier ways. But organizations whose shift structure or location leaves workers little options but fast food adopt unhealthy behaviors. While we are not responsible for the health and wellness habits of others, we can build systems and practices that support others in their quest

---

9   "Strengthen relationships for longer, healthier life," Harvard Health Publishing, Harvard Medical School, January 18, 2011. https://www.health.harvard.edu/healthbeat/strengthen-relationships-for-longer-healthier-life

to behave in healthier and more productive ways. Organizational psychologists are quickly learning that companies who care about the *community* they are building within their workforce are more likely to retain talented employees and produce a greater bottom line. As a result, companies are getting better at internally ensuring their employees' wellness and are creating external programs dedicated to social good. As society becomes more aware of the impact businesses have in our communities, employees and customers are demanding this of those the work for and support.

Our mental wellness is greatly linked to community, too. Obviously, we know we are happier and feel less anxious when we have strong relationships in our lives. But our ability to overcome trauma—or more specifically, our inability to do so—is linked to our relationships with others. For example, studies show that the effects from individual and familial trauma can be passed through generations, such as victimization from violence and war.

Collective trauma occurs when a group of people is affected by a specific event or behavior. You already know that factors such as disasters, violence, poverty, or oppression can greatly affect communities at both group and individual levels. But have you ever worked in a toxic work environment? The abusive nature of even one or two leaders can create collective trauma. The behavior or policies of an organization can trigger systemic laziness, apathy, resentment or even violence. When an employee leaves such an organization, it is not uncommon for them to experience symptoms of post-traumatic stress disorder (PTSD) and have difficulty adjusting to the new work environment.

My client Samuel[10] left a small, family-owned manufacturing firm for a position in a large company. In his previous position, yelling, cursing, blaming, and belittling were everyday occurrences. Leadership believed employees were only trying to "get one over" on them, regardless of what the employee's behavior was. They rarely (if ever) praised anyone, while publicly berating workers for the smallest infractions. Trust was corroded in both directions, and employees spent far more of their time avoiding punishment than concentrating on quality or excellence.

Samuel's new manager contacted me to coach him after he noticed some "unusual" behaviors. Samuel seemed jumpy and defensive most days and any criticism was met with steely stoicism. While he seemed confident and competent at his role, Samuel provided very little feedback to his employees. In fact, he hardly spoke to anyone. He frequently seemed agitated, on edge, and suspicious. His manager had approached him several times to discuss how he might better communicate and interact with others, to no avail.

After speaking with Samuel and learning his experience at his last company, I recognized evidence of trauma in some of his behaviors. With two small children at home and a wife who didn't work, regular threats of being fired didn't help his stress level. He was constantly hypervigilant, fearful of every move he made. For 15 years his only interactions with leaders were punitive and negative. His coping mechanism was to shut down mentally and emotionally fearing that he, like some of his colleagues in the past, would otherwise succumb to a heart attack or chronic illness.

---

10 *Name changed to protect client identity*

He finally left the company when he recognized the effect it was having on his mental health but struggled to acclimate to his new environment which was open, communicative, and embraced failure as a necessary part of growth.

It was not an easy process for Samuel to overcome his trauma and let go of ingrained assumptions, but he eventually did. What is more troubling is the thousands of individuals working in hostile or toxic environments that do not escape. Communities and organizations can make or break someone depending on the circumstances. While they are not responsible for anyone's individual behaviors or wellness, they can create environments that are supportive and productive rather than toxic and abusive.

We Are Not Broken

While the pandemic wasn't solely to blame for an international healthcare staffing shortage, the industry experienced a large rise after its onset (at the time of this book's publishing, the deficit hovers around 25%). From the onset of the pandemic, clinicians and support staff had to manage personal exposure risks and stress (and sometimes personal illness), the onslaught of patients with the virus, an upheaval of safety protocols, vaccination administration and considerations, increased emotional strain and post-traumatic stress disorder, and shortages of contracted goods such as cafeteria services and medical supplies. At a time when everyone was needed, stores of paid time off were irrelevant. Working from home wasn't an option (though Telehealth services helped relieve some offices, and it will be an important option for immobile or distant patients well into the future). Feeling burned out, unappreciated, and powerless, many workers retired or quit. Even those who hadn't reached the point of exhaustion left because there was no one to be at home while their children attended school online, or to sit with their elderly parents when home health care workers were sidelined by illness. Whatever the reason for their departure, these missing colleagues increased the already strained staff of hospitals and doctors' offices.

When I ask clinicians how they made it through this time, the leading answer, almost always with a shrug, is, "because we had to." That's the mantra of resilience. We do what we have to. But here's the thing: we don't *have* to. We could quit. We could stop caring. We could push our responsibilities onto someone else. We could dial it in. But we don't. Showing up is half the battle; the other half is finishing the race. When our community depended on it, these clinicians and staff persevered, and we're all better for it.

About a year into the pandemic, I was asked to provide resilience training for several medical groups and hospital shifts. Yes, they had made it through the toughest time, the most critical stages of contagion and risk. They had persevered. They were still standing, resilient. But they were exhausted, burned out, and defeated. My job was to explain what they were experiencing—to outline what burnout looks like, how to avoid it, and how to build inner resilience.

After one training a nurse approached me and said, "I just want to thank you. I don't feel broken anymore." My heart hurt for her (as yours likely did reading this). That's the downside of perseverance: we make it through, but at what cost? We talked for a few minutes about what she was doing to improve her self-care, and how she could fight feelings of defeat and isolation. She said, "this training helped…not just because of what you said but because I realized I'm not alone. I didn't know so many of my coworkers feel the same way." Once again, the power of community lit the spark of resilience.

Adversity comes with a price. It wears us down, makes us second-guess what we know, and depletes our relationships. Bouncing back—rebuilding our reserves—takes patience and dedication. It takes self-care, and in the case of large-scale adversity, others-centered care. The healthcare industry is now learning the importance of equipping their employees not just with individual wellness efforts but group wellness, also. They are recognizing the importance of processing trauma and adversity in group settings, sharing both the burden of struggle and strategies for overcoming. Our ability to help others feel less alone is critical to their recovery success, as it is to our own.

Sometimes we feel collectively broken. When our community or nation experiences a significant hardship—such as a natural disaster, war, mass shooting or act of terrorism, or widespread pandemic—we can feel overwhelmed by the incredible myriad of needs of our community. We are tired, emotional, and feel broken. Feeling helpless, we point fingers at those we believe are more responsible or more capable to identify solutions. It's hard to imagine how we will cope with tomorrow, much less next week. And thinking of the wellness of the next generation can feel almost unapproachable. That's when mindfulness is critical (it works at the community level, too). What can you do for your employees over the next few days? What does your school, worship center, or community need for the next month? What resources will help now, if only for today? Resilience isn't built in leaps. It's built one step at a time.

Whatever you—or your community—may be facing, you are not broken. You are not alone. And you don't have to "fix" it by yourself. In fact, in many cases, you can't. We need the help of our friends, colleagues, loved ones, and community to be our best selves. Though I am a fierce advocate for self-sufficiency and personal achievement, the reality is we never fully succeed alone. It takes the power of the whole to create the brilliant sum of its parts.

For Reflection

Answer the following questions alone or with your team:

1. Are you afraid to ask for help? Why or why not?

    a. *Does your organizational culture encourage or discourage asking for help?*

2. What fears do have about relying on others?

3. What fears do you have about others relying on you?

4. What community issues affect your daily life (such as poverty, crime, etc.)? How do you think this affects your quality of life?

5. How can you use the resources or assistance of your community to help you overcome a specific challenge?

6. What is one thing you can do to help your community?

PRINCIPLE SEVEN:

THE EXTRAORDINARY IS POSSIBLE

Hope is the pillar that holds up the world.
Hope is the dream of a waking man.

—Pliny the Elder

The Main Ingredient

In the summer of 1947, the world was introduced to the musings and life of an ordinary girl living in extraordinary circumstances. We grew to know her through her diary: a catalog of thoughts, emotions, events, and conversations held over two years in hiding during the Holocaust of World War II. She was precocious and kind and wrote about the things most teenage girls think about: her family, falling in love, her understanding of the world, her future. But it wasn't what she wrote about that captured the hearts of millions. Nearly a century later Anne Frank remains a beloved part of our collective soul because she beautifully and tragically embodied the most precious of human characteristics: **hope**.

Resilience is possible with flexibility, positivity, gratitude, self-awareness, and courage. If any of these is missing, our resilience is diluted, but we'll still make it. But resilience not possible without hope. When hope fails, so do we. **Hope is the foundation of resilience.**

Hope manifests in many ways. It becomes our faith, love, and confidence. When we can see a better future, if even momentarily, or if even for someone else, we have the one ingredient necessary to persevere. When we believe in ourselves, others, and a power greater than us all, we are able to achieve amazing things. Simply put, greatness occurs because we believe it can. We achieve because we have the vision that something is possible and the confidence that we can make it happen. We don't always know beyond doubt that we can succeed, but without this assuredness we are sure to fail.

On September 11, 2001, when four planes exploded into the World Trade Center towers, the Pentagon, and a Pennsylvania field, America was brought to its knees. This wasn't our first or greatest tragedy—we've lost millions throughout history to war, hunger, and pandemics—but this was the greatest event of adversity in our recent memory. It changed us forever and paved the way for a collective unsettledness that remains with us more than twenty years later. In the hours and days following, Americans reported a dramatic increase in prayer and religious activity. We gathered in solidarity to offer our hope to those who lost their lives and their families. We offered it to ourselves, too, for innocence lost.

Twenty years later I had the honor of meeting with four survivors of the attacks. All New Yorkers, they were at or near the World Trade Center when the first plane hit. They described the details of their day: the incredible chaos, difficulty seeing or breathing, the smells in the air, and walking many miles to get to their families. Their memories are as vivid today as they were two decades ago, because tragedy hold permanency in our minds. Fortunately, so does hope.

I asked them about their experiences and how they were able to move forward. They talked about the terror they felt not knowing who was still alive as they made their way through and out of the city. They worried whether their families were ok or if another attack was imminent. They also shared what the days were like after: sleeplessness, the guilt of survival, physical pain and tremors, grief, anger, and unthinkable sadness. But more than anything, they spoke of hope. Their hope for their children's future, hope for America, hope for the families who lost loved ones, hope for the world. That somehow, while unbeknownst in the present, we would survive. Hope is what sustained them: that we would emerge a healed nation. They had to believe this was not only possible, but promised.

All four of these survivors, though of varying religious backgrounds and practices, relied upon their belief in a greater power in the days and months that followed the attacks. This is true of nearly all the victims I have worked with over the years. They mention prayer, meditation, or gathering with others in places of worship as an important part of their healing. While it is not necessary to believe in a specific entity or dogma, my research indicates that a belief in something greater than ourselves is a critical—if not the most important—part of overcoming adversity. We instinctively feel connected to something bigger, more important, and outside ourselves. This connection is what sustains us in our most difficult moments, a lifeline to a better future.

To believe the extraordinary is possible requires us to think bigger than ourselves. It requires an awareness that remarkable things can happen with dedication, focus, and belief. It is the belief that tomorrow can be more powerful than today, and that we are capable of growth beyond our current condition. Whether your belief is in a connection to a higher power, or to the whole of humanity, your confidence that better is around the corner is paramount to your resilience.

The Case for Confidence

Only when we believe the extraordinary is possible—when we have the confidence in our abilities and in our future—are we truly capable of achieving it. Hundreds of star athletes, innovators, musicians, Nobel Prize winners, and entrepreneurs will tell you they believed in themselves when no one else did. Countless stories fill our bestselling books, movies, and news feeds of people who overcame remarkable odds because they believed they could. When the going gets tough, what, and who, do you believe in?

Those who are self-confident take more risks, have better coping skills, do better on tests, have more fulfilling relationships, and experience a myriad of other benefits. They set, and achieve, higher goals for themselves. In short, they are more resilient. Confidence is that relentless voice inside us that says, "you've got this." It enables us to envision what is possible. In fact, studies show that athletes who engage in visioning exercises—imagining themselves achieving in vivid and specific detail—perform better and more consistently. Scientists have found a positive correlation between confidence and academic achievement, athletic performance, innovation, and workforce promotions. Conversely, a lack of self-confidence is linked with anxiety, depression, aggression, and low achievement. When we don't believe in ourselves, our coping skills drop significantly. We lose our resilience.

History is replete with examples of individuals whose self-confidence made the difference between success and failure. Often, it is our darkest moment, when no one believes in us, that we're just about to launch to success. Walt Disney, a household name of remarkable achievement, experienced bankruptcy, failure, legal troubles, a nervous breakdown, and continuous rejection before becoming successful. In fact, while Disney sought financing for his business, Mickey Mouse was rejected three hundred times before someone finally said yes.[11] Thomas Edison, inventor of the lightbulb, made 1,000 unsuccessful attempts before succeeding. Albert Einstein, Michael Jordan, J.K. Rowling, Abraham Lincoln, and hundreds of other game-changers first failed (and many almost gave up) before succeeding. The common thread? They believed in themselves more than they believed in their failures.

The magic of confidence is that it doesn't require ability (that comes later). It only requires the belief in your abilities. Confidence is the thought of what is possible and the determination to act on those thoughts. It is your ideas, your vision, your conviction. It doesn't necessitate skills, resources, or special conditions, but the belief that you can develop the skills, secure the resources, or build the special conditions necessary for achievement. If you, or your team, believe you can't achieve something, you won't. Belief that you will at least gives you a 50% higher chance of it happening!

Building confidence requires dedication and time, but with effort it becomes habit. If you are struggling to find your confidence, there are research-proven ways to build it, and science is identifying more methods all the time. Take time to practice some of the following techniques to boost your confidence.

Visualize. Visualization is a powerful tool to get your mind programmed for desirable behavior. Take quiet time to think about what you want, and be very, very specific. Think about what the desired goal or behavior looks like, including what you might be doing, saying, thinking, and most importantly, thinking. For example, if you want to ace an upcoming presentation, imagine

---

11 Pak, Eudie. "Walt Disney's Rocky Road to Success," Updated June 17, 2020. Biography.com. https://www.biography.com/news/walt-disney-failures

everything about it: what you're wearing, how you sound, what you say, the expressions on the faces of your audience, how you'll move, what the room may look like, etc. But most importantly, how does it feel to do an outstanding job? Visualization is about programming your mind to the thoughts and feelings of success. Your actions will follow suit.

Say Yes. This one is for all my risk-adverse friends! For a determined time, such as thirty days, make a promise to yourself to say "yes" to opportunities that come your way. It may be a work request, social event, travel—it doesn't matter. There is a tiny, exquisite moment between "yes" and "no" in which all things are possible. Get out of the habit of saying "no" because it's complicated, time-consuming, hard work, or you're afraid. Do it anyway. You'll have some great experiences, and maybe even a couple of lousy ones. But the outcome will be a reduction in your anxiety and a boost to your confidence about doing new things.

Set Goals. This one may seem obvious, but most people don't set goals (or they only set the big ones). Research shows if we write down our goals, we're more likely to achieve them, so I recommend you do this on paper. Set small goals: for today, for this week, or things that don't take a lot of time or energy to do. The point is to make it actionable and achievable so that our minds pick up the habit. Setting tasks as a goal, rather than a "to do," frames it as a commitment and an achievement in our minds so we're more likely to tackle them. Once you've mastered small goals, give yourself some big ones: finishing your degree, redecorating your house, whatever has been on your mind. The point is, the more you set and achieve goals, the more your mind feels confident it can achieve. It doesn't matter how unimportant the goal is—your mind doesn't care. It will build confidence on the evidence of achievement.

Prepare. For all of us, we are more confident when we feel prepared. For some, it is a critical and nonnegotiable part of confidence, and can be quite unsettling if they feel unprepared. For those who place great importance in preparedness, allow yourself—without judgement—the time necessary to feel ready to take on a task, event, or change. Don't worry about the amount of time—release that thought and do what feels right. Over time, as your confidence builds, you'll notice you need less time to prepare. If the situation does not allow for ample preparation, prepare mentally and emotionally for your response. How will you handle feelings of ambiguity? How will you answer questions you don't know the answer for? Walk through the "what ifs" so that you have a plan for the unexpected.

Seek learning. When failure or disappointment occurs, and it inevitably will, seek what can be learned from it. Immediately release judgement and home in on why it failed, what specifically didn't work, and how you might do it differently if given the opportunity. Be specific about personal growth: what did this show you about your personal behaviors? What, if anything, would you like to fix or learn better for the future? Is there a skill or behavior you'd like to improve, or a method you'd like to try instead? When we reframe failure into learning, it is failing forward. We're giving ourselves the opportunity for the failure to be useful, and it signals our brain to seek pertinent information for growth. By focusing on what can be learned you are creating a mindset of confidence: I can accept this failure because it gives me useful information to succeed in the future.

Ask Questions. Inquiry is one of the greatest gifts you can give yourself and your confidence. When we ask questions, and sit with questions rather than seeking answers, we unhinge ourselves from the narrow expectations of solution-based thinking. Our brains begin to seek more information, more options, and better resources. We become more confident as we recognize the multitude of solutions available to us. Asking questions rather than seeking answers also makes us humble. That may sound like the opposite of confidence, but it's not: true confidence is the ability to sit comfortably in the unknown and know we'll emerge successful. The more we ponder, reflect, and inquire, the more our minds access new and different information. Inquiry provides the power to gather a wide range of ideas so that we are more confident in the solutions we've identified.

Get Things Done. The more productive we are, the more confident we are. It's that simple. We are made to move, to be productive: our bodies and minds are set on "go" the minute we wake up. While rest and relaxation are essential for our health, too much of it can be toxic and lead to depression. When we achieve even small things, our mind recognizes it as a reward and seeks more. If you can achieve at least three things daily—no matter how small—you will see an increase in your confidence.

Focus on Strengths. This isn't about ignoring your weaknesses—it's about acknowledging your strengths. What are you good at? What do you do that seems easy, that you can do without even thinking, that others seem to struggle with? That's your strength. Maybe you're a good listener. Or you are a strategic thinker. Maybe you're great at identifying risk or providing context to situations. Whatever it is, it has an equal and opposite weakness that can make us feel like we're failing somehow. The challenge is not to get down about what you lack but build upon what you have. For example, you might find that your feelings get hurt easily, but this may be because you are a sensitive person who others find compassionate and empathetic. Those are great strengths! You might have great difficulty being patient in brainstorming meetings or with processes that take too long because you are natural driver who helps others accomplish a lot. Recognize that being good in one area may mean we have work to do in another. Be willing to release the shame of what you aren't and celebrate the gift of what you are.

Do the Next Right Thing. For many of us, reflecting on the full picture of our lives, and what may be required for our success, is overwhelming. We can't see how our efforts today might gain benefits into the future, so we lose ground in our decisions. It doesn't have to be this way. You are only responsible for doing the next right thing, right now. Today. Your daily mission isn't to be any lofty ideal; it's to live into that ideal day by day, decision by decision. If we focus on what the next right decision is, letting go of what our previous decisions have been or what the future may hold, we build confidence in our personal power. Act what you know is right, not to be right. Because acting with integrity is confidence. Acting with impunity is hubris.

Imposter Syndrome

Tonya[12] is a bright attorney who was recently promoted to Partner in her firm. As we met over lunch to celebrate her achievement, I noticed she seemed somewhat reticent to discuss it. Tonya is a fierce advocate for her clients, with a reputation of going (many) extra miles to win her cases. She has a reputation of excellence and integrity that proceeds her to the courtroom. So, it was not surprising that she had been promoted or that her firm had such confidence in her abilities. I thought about this as she sat with her face perched in one hand, pushing pasta around her plate with her fork in the other.

"I'm not sure I'm up to this challenge," she was saying. "I didn't go to an Ivy League school. I wasn't even sure I'd pass the bar. And now my partners want me to charge more, but I don't feel like I've earned it," she said quietly.

"Are their hourly rates higher than yours?" I asked. She nodded. "Well, it's fair that they'd want you to bring in the same as a partner. Why don't you think you've earned it?"

"I'm five years behind most of them. And my area is so special-ized—most of them can handle a wider variety of cases than I can. I don't know…it just seems like I'm constantly trying to prove my worth. Like no matter how hard I try, I'm not as knowledgeable or capable as everyone around me."

Ouch. I've been there. And if you're being honest, so have you. We all doubt our abilities, experience, and worthiness from time to time. It's human (and in some ways, it keeps us humble). Tonya was

---

12   *Name has been changed to protect identity*

experiencing a normal reaction to a new challenge. But for her, it ran deeper.

"How long have you felt this way?" I asked. "Meaning, is this because they named you Partner?"

"No," she sighed. "I've felt this way my entire career."

"Ah. It sounds like you might be fighting Imposter Syndrome. That's not easy," I said. Imposter Syndrome is a phenomenon experienced by people who feel they are less capable than the persona seen by others. They don't believe they are as good, capable, or smart as others might believe. In other words, that despite great appearances, they may in fact be a fraud.

"I think so," she said, recognizing the term. "But I don't know what to do about it. It's so bad that I think about leaving the firm more often than I'd like to admit."

"What good would that do for you?" I asked. "Would you be happier or more fulfilled in a different role or career?"

"No," she said thoughtfully. "I love what I do. And I've worked my entire career to get here. I just don't like this feeling."

"No one does, but thankfully, you can overcome it," I said. "Can you view your qualifications differently, perhaps as others do? For example, you have a narrow focus of law expertise. That's a good thing: it makes you an expert in an area not many others are. It's what makes you so great in the courtroom, though it may be something very specific, you know everything about that one thing," I explained. "And you may be five years behind others, but you've got a great record of winning. That means something. And you didn't go to an ivy league school, who cares? Has that stopped you from being a great attorney?"

"No," she smiled. "No one even mentions it. I just think about it when the guys talk about their school days."

"There you go," I said. "What I'm more concerned about is why you think you have to be perfect."

She laughed and said, "says the recovering perfectionist?" (Yeah, my friends know this about me). We spent time discussing what she was experiencing. Imposter Syndrome occurs to high-achieving people who are always striving for better, more, higher. To drive ourselves towards achievement is a great quality, unless to do so is borne of a fear of failure and imperfection. Then we find it impossible to ever be fully satisfied with our achievements. It is possible—likely, even—that we are every bit as capable as others believe we are. And maybe not. It doesn't matter. What matters is what we believe about ourselves.

Perfectionism is confidence's nemesis. It keeps us from trying new things or accepting the unavoidable trial-and-error process of life. Imposter Syndrome is perfectionism on overload, having taken root over months or years. When we doubt our qualifications and abilities, we hold ourselves back. We lose our sense of deserv-edness. Meanwhile, those around us—who might be less capable than we are—are achieving more. Have you ever seen someone in a role you would like and thought, "how in the world did that person get there? I could do better than that!" That's what it feels like to be sidelined by Imposter Syndrome.

If you feel like you don't belong somewhere, challenge yourself to discover why. Is it your personal qualities, or the qualities of the environment you're in? Are you restricted by your own capabilities, or the narrow expectations of a system (for example, you may be fully capable, have a degree, and be the best fit for the position, but not the specific degree desired by the hiring agent). While it may be that you need to spruce up on some skills or characteristics, it is equally likely that you're placing unnecessary expectations on yourself. Confident people don't worry about what they lack, they utilize what they excel at. Take time to recognize your unique qualities and how you personally contribute to your environment. Focus on building your confidence around all you've accomplished. And know that, for all the great qualities others may possess, they too are human. They also experience disappointment and self-doubt. The only difference between those who fail and those who succeed is when that self-doubt kicks in, the successful choose to move forward anyway.

EXERCISE: VALUES-BASED LIVING

Resilient people know themselves. You know this already, but it bears repeating. They know their strengths, their weaknesses, their goals, their fears. But most importantly, they know what's important to them. These are nonnegotiable, permanent values that drive their thoughts and actions. In other words, resilient people live values-based lives.

To live from our values means we must first identify them. Think for a moment about what is most important to you. What is most important for you to convey in an important conversation? How do you approach problem-solving? What qualities do you like most in your closest friends? These questions may help you think about the words that define your core values. Write a few of them down, then choose 3-4 that are most important to you. (If helpful, use the list below for some ideas.)

Respect	Empathy	Responsibility
Honesty	Courage	Humility
Loyalty	Integrity	Harmony
Optimism	Wisdom	Efficiency
Humor	Consistency	Intelligence
Creativity	Compassion	Transparency

Next, define how you recognize those values. You'll find that you may have different ideas than others about how you express your values. For example, you may choose "respect" as one of your values. For most people, being on time for a meeting is a sign of respect. But how do you define "on time?" If you've set a meeting with someone for 9:00 a.m., you might answer, "a few minutes before 9:00." Or you might say, "around 9:00" (which could include 9:01, which may be seen as disrespectful to the person who answered "a few minutes before 9:00"). As silly as this example might seem, I see people get angry about time differences all the time!

How we express our values is as important as the values we hold. Most of us would say that honesty is one of our top values. But when it comes time to be honest, how willing are you to uphold that value? Are you willing to tell a friend that they look terrible in their favorite outfit? Ah…now you're discovering you have a conflicting value of supporting the feelings of people you care about. In this scenario, which value wins?

The point is, your values will compete from time to time, or you'll discover that you place differing importance on them. The challenge is to know, at a baseline, what you value most so that you can make decisions that best reflect who you are and what you want. Confidence occurs when we have a deep understanding of what is most important to us and base our thoughts, actions, and decisions on those factors.

Has someone ever repeated something you said or did and you thought, that doesn't sound like me at all? Or, conversely, yep. I don't remember saying that, but I believe I did! That's what it feels like when you know your values well. You know what your reactions are likely be in most circumstances, and you are confident in your consistency. When you know what your values are, you begin living them. That stability is imperative to your resilience.

Stop Freaking Out!

You heard me. If you want to be more resilient, stop freaking out! Our world is on emotional overdrive. We are addicted to controversy and outrage. Our social media feeds, news, and conversations are tinged with negativity and alarm. News stations clamor to cover stories that are a little more salacious than the yesterday's. And our schools and organizations are exhausted by the burden of addressing people's wellness in addition to their education or productivity. We are collectively wearing ourselves out.

Our brains love outrage. It's like a drug, sending reward signals every time we give ourselves a hit of self-righteousness. As others reinforce our thoughts and behaviors (such as through "likes" on social media), they too are giving us hits of cortisol and reward.

Over time these "hits" diminish the ability of our brains to function normally, eventually resulting in lowered judgement, immune suppression, and reduced ability to create memories.[13] It is our responsibility to ourselves and others to weigh facts, filter our emotional responses, and react in healthy and proactive ways.

Confidence in your thoughts and actions is a result of practice. It may take several tries before you intuitively know when your reaction fits the scenario. But there are steps you can take each time to get information (and therefore your reaction) right. When you're faced with a challenge or negative information, ask yourself three important questions:

1. **Does this sound right?** If the story, headline, conversation, rumor, etc. doesn't make sense to you, you're likely missing critical information. Think of a time when you learned of someone's behavior and thought, "who would do such a thing?!" If you're asking that, the answer is probably no one you know. It's more likely you're missing some key information. While occasionally (if not rarely) it turns out we're dealing with someone who has nefarious or illogical motives, most of the time when you dig a little deeper, you'll find something that helps it make sense. We're only as trustworthy as our actions. Take a moment to make sure your actions reflect good information and decision-making.

2. **Will this matter later?** We tend to react emotionally to things happening in the moment that, upon reflection,

---

13 "How Anger Affects the Brain and Body," National Institute for the Clinical Application of Behavioral Medicine, 2017. https://www.nicabm.com/how-anger-affects-the-brain-and-body-infographic/

we won't care about in a year (or even a week!). What impact will this event, rumor, conversation, or circumstances have on you in the future? Will you care? If not, let it go—it's not worth your peace. If it will matter in the future, act only on what can you do to mitigate the problem. Any more or less and you are sacrificing your resilience.

3. **What is the worst-case scenario?** What doesn't kill us makes us stronger? Not always. But what doesn't kill us is survivable. What's the worst that can come of the information or circumstances you've been given? Think through the worst possible scenario. Take it all the way in your mind until it ends in ruin. How are you? How will you survive? What will you do then? Resilience is confidence in your ability to stand against adversity, and to come back strong. Know that you are capable of withstanding anything you put your mind to, especially with the help of others.

When my colleagues and I surveyed two hundred employees to ask which characteristics instill the most trust in their leaders, the ability to calmly and confidently respond to adversity ranked second (only behind honesty). We look to leaders for their strengths: not just in technical skills and experience, but in their ability to emotionally withstand challenges. We anticipate following their lead so it's imperative they know how to appropriately respond to crisis. Today's fast-changing climate of social media and news make this difficult: weathering a public relations crisis is a top concern for most managers and CEOs. Leaders must respond to market changes, recessions, recalls, interpersonal conflicts, customer issues, and staffing shortages. Whatever the crisis, they have to be confident in their ability to manage and overcome.

When you receive information that you don't like, have a conversation that goes badly, or learn of an impending problem, stop. Breathe. Think about how this will affect you and others, and whether the impact is temporary. Think about your reaction, including how you will share the information with others. If a conversation isn't going well, wait until you are calm enough to hold it. Ask yourself whether you want to get your point across or prove you are right, or whether your goal is to help the other person and your relationship. Will you "share" the negative post or email? Or will you take a moment to think about why it matters, who it matters to, and whether it should be shared?

And if you do freak out a bit, own it. I've seen leaders responding to legitimate crises who yell, cry, shut down, and storm out. While they are dealing with real and difficult circumstances, they may not have behaved in a proactive way. They're human, after all. Whether it's in front of children we don't want to scare, friends we don't want to appear weak in front of, or employees we don't want to lose ground with, we've all had moments in which we reacted before thinking and regretted it later. In other words, we've all freaked out. The bigger problem is when we try to deny or ignore that our behavior wasn't what we wanted it to be (by the way, we're fooling no one). Explain what you were experiencing in that moment. Allow your vulnerability to show. Everyone knows what was happening for us anyway, so owning it will allow others' understanding and respect.

Hope, Confidence, Resilience

Your path to resilience relies heavily on your ability to believe in what is possible. Look to the small miracles around you: the entrepreneur who built a business empire from $40 to their name. The soldier who saved dozens of lives with a bullet in his leg. The friend who has overcome cancer—twice. Tremendous and extraordinary things happen every day if we're willing to look for them. This attitude—one of seeking the extraordinary—helps build your confidence in yourself, others, and a higher power that all things are indeed possible. It sustains us when we're not sure of the outcome of our circumstances. Remember: hope is the foundation of resilience. Be intimately connected to what you hope for, what you believe in. It will make all the difference in your ability to lead, achieve, and succeed.

For Reflection

1. What one thing will I do today to increase my confidence?
2. What do you hope for? How do these hopes shape your outlook of the world?
3. Who inspires you? List at least three people—living or passed—that inspire you with their achievements, character, or personality. Why do you find them inspiring? More importantly, how will you develop or articulate similar characteristics?

4. What does the word "perseverance" mean to you? How do you embody it?
5. What one thing (or person) amazed you today?

WHAT'S NEXT: WALKING THE RESILIENT PATH

Resilience begins and ends with our ability to believe we are more than the sum of our circumstances. To know we are capable of anything we set our minds to and to find the resources necessary to make that happen. It is about survival, grit, confidence, and thriving. It's not easy, but it's always possible.

Now that you've discovered the key characteristics of a resilient person—courage, self-awareness, optimism, gratitude, flexibility, purpose, and hope—you are ready to act resiliently. While these characteristics look different in each of us, my research has assured one thing: anyone who possesses these characteristics is capable of true resilience.

Resilience is not a one-time option. It's not something we develop within ourselves and then walk away from. It takes focus, self-care, and continuous improvement. That doesn't mean we have to think about it constantly; it's more like the settings running in the background of our mind's computer. Occasionally, when there's a critical issue, it will pop up and demand attention. But we must provide ongoing maintenance, attention, and updates to keep it working optimally. If we maintain it well it will kick in and mitigate issues when it's needed.

Think daily about one or more of these characteristics and how you are exhibiting them, ensuring you don't lose sight of them in the chaos of life. The best way to ensure you are tending to your resilience is to engage in self-care. It's nonnegotiable: if we are not maintaining ourselves, we have nothing to offer when challenges arise. Exercise, eat healthily, get enough sleep, take time for reflection, pay your bills, complete your tasks. Self-care isn't always glamorous. It's doing whatever is necessary to live into our best selves, including meeting our responsibilities.

Be unflinchingly dedicated to self-care. Not getting enough sleep? Get a sleep test, turn screens off at a reasonable time, or exercise daily to wear out your body. No time for exercise? Make it! You have ten minutes here or there. Utilize them. Bottom line: if it's important, you will find a way. There are no excuses in self-care.

As you pay more attention to how you embody the characteristics of resilience, be patient and kind to yourself. It's an ongoing process, one that even the experts haven't mastered. Each challenge or crisis we face is different, requiring different solutions from us. We'll mess up. We'll be lazy. We'll avoid. And we'll feel discouraged. And then we'll get back in there because that's what we're called to do when things get tough.

As you help others discover their resilience, be patient and kind for them, too. They are learning. They are taking risks they haven't taken before. The path to resilience is vulnerable and personal. It requires us to examine the deepest parts of our minds and hearts. And it requires us to emerge better. It's not easy, but it is exceptionally worth it.

You are capable of resilience. We all are. Find what inspires you, what gives you purpose, what drives you to want to overcome. Invest in those things, and in yourself, with time and effort. And most of all, enjoy the journey. Love what you learn about yourself and relish every single moment in which you discover that you are more capable than you believed.

ADDITIONAL RESOURCES

1. Lieberman, Daniel E.; Mahaffey, Mickey; Cubesare Quimare, Silvino; Holowka, Nicholas B.; Wallace, Ian J.; Baggish, Aaron L. (June 2020). "Running in Tarahumara (Rarámuri) Culture: Persistence Hunting, Footracing, Dancing, Work, and the Fallacy of the Athletic Savage." *Current Anthropology*, Volume 61, Number 3. https://www.journals.uchicago.edu/doi/full/10.1086/708810

2. "Reconditioning the brain to overcome fear." *University of Cambridge Research*, 21 November 2016. https://www.cam.ac.uk/research/news/reconditioning-the-brain-to-overcome-fear

3. Cantarigiu, Ramona; Hadad, Shahrazad (September 2013). "The Importance of Play in Overcoming Fears of Entrepreneurial Failure." *European Conference on Knowledge Management; Kidmore End*. https://www.proquest.com/openview/8ec61d4f2aacd1985cc6652ec0f140ae/1?pq-origsite=gscholar&cbl=1796412

4. Ranganathan, Vinoth K., Siemionow, Vlodek, Liu, Jing Z, Sahgal, Vinod, Yue, Guang H. (2004). "From mental power to muscle power—gaining strength by using the mind." Neuropsychologia, Volume 42, Issue 42, Pages 944-956. https://doi.org/10.1016/j.neuropsychologia.2003.11.018

5. Graham, Linda (posted September 15, 2019). "Train your brain to Build Resilience." *Mindful: healthy mind, healthy life*. https://www.mindful.org/train-your-brain-to-build-resilience

6. Vieselmeyer, J., Holguin, J., & Mezulis, A. (2017). "The role of resilience and gratitude in posttraumatic stress and growth following a campus shooting." *Psychological Trauma: Theory, Research, Practice, and Policy*, 9(1), 62–69.

7. Claro, Susana, Paunesku, David, Dweck, Carol S. "Growth mindset tempers the effects of poverty on academic achievement." *PNAS*. Contributed by Carol S. Dweck, May 25, 2016; posted July 18, 2016. https://www.pnas.org/doi/abs/10.1073/pnas.1608207113

8. Jamieson, Jeremy P., Crum, Alia J., Goyer, J. Parker, Marotta, Marisa E., Akinola, Modupe (22 February 2018). "Optimizing stress responses with reappraisal and mindset interventions: an integrated model." *Anxiety, Stress & Coping: An International Journal*. Volume 31, 2018-Issue 3. https://www.tandfonline.com/doi/abs/10.1080/10615806.2018.1442615

9. Pratt, Misty (posted February 17, 2022). "The Science of Gratitude." *Mindful: healthy mind, healthy life*. https://www.mindful.org/the-science-of-gratitude

10. Unanue, Wenceslao, Esteban Gomez Mella, Marcos, Cortez, Diego Alejandro, Bravo, Diego, Araya-Véliz, Claudio, Unanue, Jesús, Van Den Broeck, Anja (8 November 2019). "The Reciprocal Relationship Between Gratitude and Life Satisfaction: Evidence From Two

Longitudinal Field Studies." *Frontiers in Psychology, Sec. Personality and Social Psychology.* https://www.frontiersin. org/articles/10.3389/fpsyg.2019.02480/full

11. Morin, Amy (posted November 23, 2014). "7 Scientifically Proven Benefits of Gratitude that Will Motivate you to Give You Thanks Year-Round." *Forbes.com.* https://www. forbes.com/sites/amymorin/2014/11/23/7-scientifically-proven-benefits-of-gratitude-that-will-motivate-you-to-give-thanks-year-round/?sh=7733a520183c

12. Fredrickson, B. L., Tugade, M. M., Waugh, C. E., & Larkin, G. R. (2003). What good are positive emotions in crisis? A prospective study of resilience and emotions following the terrorist attacks on the United States on September 11th, 2001. *Journal of Personality and Social Psychology, 84*(2), 365–376. https://doi. org/10.1037/0022-3514.84.2.365

13. Contie, Vicki (June 22, 2007). "Brain Imaging Reveals Joys of Giving." *NIH Research Matters.* https:// www.nih.gov/news-events/nih-research-matters/brain-imaging-reveals-joys-giving

14. Weisner, Lauren (July 2020). "Individual and Community Trauma: Individual Experiences in Collective Environments." *Illinois Criminal Justice Information Authority.* https://icjia.illinois.gov/researchhub/articles/individual-and-community-trauma-individual-experi-ences-in-collective-environments

15. Stenger, Marianne (posted April 10, 2017). "7 Ways to Develop Cognitive Flexibility." *informED.*

https://www.opencolleges.edu.au/informed/
features/7-ways-develop-cognitive-flexibility

16. Markway, Barbara (posted September 20, 2018).
    "Why Self-Confidence is More Important Than you
    Think." *Psychology Today*. https://www.psycholo-
    gytoday.com/us/blog/shyness-is-nice/201809/
    why-self-confidence-is-more-important-you-think

17. Warrell, Margie (posted February 26, 2015). "Use It Or
    Lose It: The Science Behind Self-Confidence." *Forbes.com*.
    https://www.forbes.com/sites/margiewarrell/2015/02/26/
    build-self-confidence-5strategies/?sh=6af0943d6ade

18. Sutton, Jeremy (posted 24 September 2020). "Self-
    Esteem Research: 20 Most Fascinating Findings."
    PositivePsychology.com. https://positivepsychology.com/
    self-esteem-research

ABOUT THE AUTHOR

JULIE H. LAWSON is an entrepreneur, author, and podcaster with more than 20 years' experience in nonprofit management and leadership development. She is the CEO of Reins Institute (reinsinstitute.com), a leadership development and coaching firm dedicated to building resilience in the workforce. To find out more about Julie and her current projects, please use the QR Code below: